THE AMERICAN NEGRO

HIS HISTORY AND LITERATURE

MYRTILLA MINER: A MEMOIR

Ellen M. O'Connor

*

THE SCHOOL FOR COLORED GIRLS

Myrtilla Miner

ARNO PRESS and THE NEW YORK TIMES
NEW YORK 1969

Reprint edition 1969 by Arno Press, Inc.
Introduction copyright © 1969 by Arno Press, Inc.

*

Library of Congress Catalog Card No. 73–92235

*

The School for Colored Girls is reprinted from a copy in the
Howard University Library

Myrtilla Miner: A Memoir is reprinted from a copy in the
State Historical Society of Wisconsin Library

*

Manufactured in the United States of America

General Editor
WILLIAM LOREN KATZ

MYRTILLA MINER HAS BEEN ONE OF THE forgotten heroines in the fight for Negro education. Yet she eminently deserves the tribute of later generations as a pioneer in a field of education which was a wilderness in her time. Myrtilla Miner, a white woman from upstate New York, established a Normal School for free Negro girls in Washington, D.C. in 1851 with but one hundred dollars—raised with difficulty—in her possession. She invaded Washington, D.C., a stronghold of pro-slavery and anti-Negro sentiment, with the aim of preparing Negro girls to become teachers of their race.

Daughter of a poor family, frail in body but staunch in spirit, Myrtilla Miner had fought for her own education in her youth with the same fervor and self-sacrifice she showed in her fight for the education of Negro girls later. She succeeded in both against great odds.

Myrtilla (who was called Myrtle by her

family and friends) was born in the town of Brookfield, Madison County, New York, in 1815. She was one of ten or twelve children of Seth and Eleanor Smith Miner. Her father was a farmer, who because of his large family and limited finances, could not afford to give Myrtilla the formal education she desired. Yet she had access to some books, for the village library was housed in the Miner home.[1]

When Myrtilla was about sixteen she taught in a small school near her home. Later she attended, for a short time, the Young Ladies Domestic Seminary at Clinton, New York. Rather frail in health even then, Myrtilla could not follow the required regime of manual labor— working for her room and board. In her short stay at the school, however, she first came to know of the lives and problems of the Negro from three Negro girls who were her schoolmates.

Attaining her goal, Myrtilla became a teacher, obtaining a position in Rochester, New York at the Clover Street Academy and later in Providence, Rhode Island. While in Providence, she became so interested in the problem of slavery that she decided to gain first-hand knowledge by teaching in the South.

With her usual determination she secured the position she wanted. During 1847 and 1848 she was the teacher of wealthy planters' daughters in the Newton Female Institute at Whitesville, Mississippi. This was her first contact with the horrible institution of slavery, and it not only reinforced her abolitionist sympathies, but also led her to attempt to teach the slave children in her spare time.

There are two versions of the incident which made her decide to teach Negroes in the North. According to Henry G. Wells, who based his account on a manuscript written by Myrtilla Miner, she asked the principal of the school "if she might teach colored children in her spare hours. He informed her that it would be impossible for her to do so as it would violate the laws of the State; that if she wished to ameliorate the condition of colored people she should work with such persons in her own section of the country where 'Northern philanthropists had a vast work to do at home to elevate their own colored people.'" Dr. Pharis, the principal of the Mississippi school, had even worked out a plan for emancipation which Myrtilla forwarded to Gerrit Smith, an abolitionist.[2]

In Ellen O'Connor's account of the incident

(based on what Myrtilla Miner told her), Myrtilla asked a planter, whose daughters she was instructing, for permission to teach the slaves on his plantation. In answer he cited the law of the State, but also suggested that she teach Negroes in the North in much cruder fashion than the principal had used. The slave-owner asked Miss Miner sarcastically, "Why don't you go *North* and teach the 'niggers,' if you are so anxious to do it?" Myrtilla took his insulting rebuff as a challenge, and did just that.[3]

She heroically overcame the difficulties of raising money, carrying on despite ill health, and danger from the stones thrown by neighborhood rowdies.

Even Frederick Douglass, whom she called on early in her enterprise, discouraged her: "As I look back to the moral surroundings of the time and place when that school was begun, and the state of public sentiment which then existed in the North as well as in the South," he wrote; "when I remember how low the estimation in which colored people were then held, how little sympathy there was with any effort to dispel their ignorance, diminish their hardships, alleviate their suffering, or soften their misfortunes,

I marvel all the more at the thought, the zeal, the faith, and the courage of Myrtilla Miner in daring to be the pioneer of such a movement for education here, in the District of Columbia, the very citadel of slavery, the place most zealously watched and guarded by the slave power, and where humane tendencies were most speedily detected and sternly opposed. . . . To me the proposition was reckless, almost to the point of madness. In my fancy, I saw this fragile little woman harassed by the law, insulted in the street, a victim of slaveholding malice, and, possibly beaten down by the mob. The fate of Prudence Crandall in Connecticut and the then recent case of Mrs. Douglass at Norfolk were before me; also my own experience in attempting to teach a Sunday-school in St. Michael's; and I dreaded the experience which, I feared, awaited Miss Miner." [4]

Frederick Douglass's words proved to be prophetic, when after teaching near her home in 1849 and 1850, Myrtilla set forth for Washington and founded her school in 1851. In its first three years the school had to move three times. Its first quarters were in a room about fourteen feet square in the home of a Negro resident of Washington, Edward C. Younger. When the number of students grew from six to forty, Miss Miner had to seek larger quarters. The next two moves were to the homes of white people in white neighborhoods. Here the teacher and her pupils were subject to harassment and persecution.

It was clear that the school needed a building of its own, and by 1853 Myrtilla Miner, through writing articles in the press, enlisting the aid of friends, and traveling North to make personal appeals, was able to raise the funds needed to buy five acres of land and a house which could serve as a schoolhouse. One-fourth of the sum of $4,000 was contributed by Harriet Beecher Stowe from her earnings from *Uncle Tom's Cabin*.

The new building, however, did not solve the problems of the school in relation to the neighbors or the powers-that-were in Washington. Myrtilla Miner had to practice pistol-shooting to discourage her enemies in the neighborhood.

Not only rowdies and ruffians were opposed to the school. Even a mayor of the city wrote against her plan to educate Negro girls, using as his arguments that they would be educated above their station, and that the presence of the school would attract more Negroes to the city.

An illustration of the hazards which lay even in sympathizing with the school, is the case of Dr. L. D. Gale, who was a chemical examiner at the United States Patent Office and had been a partner of Samuel F. B. Morse and Alfred Vail in the development of the electric telegraph. "In 1857 the *National Intelligencer* had published an article attacking the Miner School and mentioned Dr. Gale as a supporter. As a consequence, he was dismissed from the Patent Office."[5]

Antagonism to the school did not subside. On May 13, 1860, Myrtilla wrote to some friends: "About one o'clock I was awakened by the sound of cracking fire. . . . I opened the door leading from my chamber and smelled smoke. . . . I screamed 'Fire!' with awful fury and then with a pail I ran for water, the fire having just that instant broken out. Then neighbors came and going out onto the roof allayed the flames. . . . For a year I had expected this, so, it did not take me unawares, but for the last year ruffians had been so quiet that I thought they had given me up."[6]

The fire, having been spotted in time, did not succeed in destroying the school. It took a larger conflagration—one which involved the nation —to do that. In 1861, a time of strife and controversy in Washington, Myrtilla again had to leave in the hope of restoring her health. She went to California. On earlier occasions when its founder had to leave, the school continued under the direction of Miss Emily Howland of Cayuga County, New York, with Miss Emma Brown, a young graduate of the Miner School, as her assistant. At this time, however, the school had to be closed.

Nevertheless, Miss Miner's friends continued to press her cause. In 1863 Congress passed an act to incorporate the Institution for the Education of Colored Youth in the District of Columbia. The legislation was due to the efforts of Senator (later Vice-President) Henry Wilson of Massachusetts, who had long been a supporter of the Miner School. Passage had had to wait, however, until Secession, when the voices of the southern senators were no longer heard. The incorporators named in the act were Henry Addison, John C. Underwood, George C. Abbot, William H. Channing (the Unitarian minister), Nancy Johnson, and Myrtilla Miner.

This was a major triumph, but Myrtilla could not savor it for long. In California she met with an accident, and returned to the home of her friend, Mrs. Nancy Johnson, in Washington. Ten days later she died. During those last few days, a friend of Mrs. Johnson's, Ellen O'Connor, spent hours with her, talking about her work, taking care of her correspondence, and beginning a formal involvement with the Miner School that culminated in her biographical memoir of Myrtilla Miner twenty-one years later.

In her memoir Ellen O'Connor tells the subsequent history of the school. It remained closed until 1871, when it merged with Howard University, establishing within the University both a preparatory and a normal (teacher-training) department. These departments were supported by the income of the Miner Fund. The plot of land purchased in 1853 for $4,000 was sold for $40,000 in 1872. Upon investment, the Fund earned an income of $3,000 per year. In 1874, the President of Howard University wrote in his annual report that the stated arrangement with the Miner Fund had been "flourishing and successful" and that he hoped it would continue.[7]

However, in 1875, the trustees of the Miner

Fund (of whom Ellen O'Connor was one) decided that the school could best carry out the intentions of its founder by being independent, and severed connections with Howard University. Wishing to keep Myrtilla Miner's memory alive, Howard University named its women's building "Miner Hall."

At about this time, Ellen O'Connor conceived the idea of writing the memoir, and wrote to various people for information about Miss Miner. Her letters to Mr. Isaac Miner, a brother, and Mrs. Albe, a niece, are in the Library of Congress.

A new building for the Miner School was dedicated by Rev. William Henry Channing in 1877. Frederick Douglass spoke eloquently at the exercises. Two years later this school— Miner Normal School—became part of the District of Columbia school system, with some administrative powers to be shared by the school system and the trustees of the Miner School (George P. Baker and Ellen O'Connor representing the Miner School). Evidently the trustees took their duties seriously. Ellen O'Connor's daughter, Jeannie, wrote to her cousin, Grace Channing, on June 5, 1882 about "mamma's school affairs. . . . Tonight she examined the examination papers for candidates for next year. There are nineteen who have passed."[8]

The Miner School became completely absorbed into the District of Columbia school system in 1885, the year of the memoir. The Miner Fund continued, however, to support Negro education.

Ellen O'Connor evidently sent a copy of the completed Memoir to Mr. Isaac Miner. On March 28, 1886, she wrote to him, saying, "I am glad you liked the memoir of your sister. I loved her very much, & felt that the story of her heroic labors here ought to be told." She also acknowledged his consent to have Myrtilla Miner's remains moved to another spot in the Oak Hill Cemetery so that a monument could be erected.[9]

In 1914, sixty-three years after the first Miner School was established with six pupils and a teacher in Mr. Younger's parlor, Congress appropriated $4,000 for a school site and $200,000 for a school building to be erected on Georgia Avenue near Euclid Avenue, in Washington, D.C.[10]

Ellen M. O'Connor (née Ellen Tarr), author of the memoir which keeps Myrtilla Miner's memory alive today, was not a professional writer. Writing as the secretary of the Institution for Colored Youth, she rarely brings herself into the narrative. She was, however, a very interesting person, whose life may have touched Myrtilla Miner's at several points before their close friendship at the time of Miss Miner's last illness.[11] She could well sympathize with the aspirations of the girls whom Myrtilla Miner wished to educate. She, too, had struggled to obtain an education, because her parents were poor, and her father ill during her early years. When a child, she had helped her mother, who had had to take in laundry, by calling for and delivering the bundles before school, her mittenless hands freezing in the icy New England mornings. While still in elementary school, she worked at stripping tobacco leaves. After her father's death, the family moved to Lowell, Massachusetts, where Ellen worked in the mills, obtaining an education from lecturers who used to come to Lowell, and from reading and discussions.

Through some friends, Ellen and her older

sister Mary Jane (Jeannie), who later became the wife of Dr. William Francis Channing, were enabled to go to a Normal School in Newton, Massachusetts. Upon graduation her sister became a teacher, and Ellen a governess in the home of Gamaliel Bailey in Washington, D.C. Here she met many leaders in the antislavery movement, for Dr. Bailey was editor of the *National Era,* the weekly organ of the American and Foreign Anti-Slavery Society. As governess, Ellen was not in a servile position; "Grace Greenwood," writing of the Bailey home, mentioned the "merry, yet intellectual, young ladies who did so much to render the Bailey *salon* so charming"—among them "the graceful Nellie Tarr."[12]

Later Ellen worked in Boston on William Lloyd Garrison's abolitionist paper, *The Liberator.* She was a friend of Paulina Wright Davis, the Woman's Rights leader, at whose home in Providence, Rhode Island, Myrtilla Miner met one of the benefactors of her school.

Ellen's marriage to William Douglas O'Connor strengthened her ties to the antislavery movement. In 1860 O'Connor's novel *Harrington* appeared, in which the author described

events in the fugitive slave rescues in Boston—
events in which he had been a participant.

The O'Connors moved to Washington in
1861. Known in his own day as a brilliant short
story writer, novelist, poet, and pamphleteer,
William Douglas O'Connor is remembered to-
day only for his friendship for and defense of
Walt Whitman.

When Whitman came to Washington in December, 1862, after having published three
editions of *Leaves of Grass,* which had gained
but scant recognition, the O'Connors found him
a room in the boarding house in which they
lived, and invited him to take his meals with
them, without cost to him. William also helped
him to find a job as copyist in the office of the
Army paymaster.

Several years later, with O'Connor's help,
Whitman became a clerk in the Treasury Department. After six months (June, 1865) Whitman was summarily dismissed because his superior saw a copy of *Leaves of Grass* in his desk,
and thought it an immoral book.

O'Connor not only set about finding him
another job, but also wrote a brilliant monograph in defense of *Leaves of Grass* and of free-

dom in letters. The title of the monograph, *The Good Gray Poet* has remained synonymous with Walt Whitman's name.

Ellen O'Connor remained Walt Whitman's friend throughout his life, even during a period of ten years when her husband and Whitman were estranged.[13] Her only published works, aside from her memoir of Myrtilla Miner, are three articles about Whitman, two in the *Conservator* in March, 1897 and May, 1906, and another in the *Atlantic Monthly* in June, 1907.[14] These appeared long after the deaths of William O'Connor (1889) and Walt Whitman (1892), and after Ellen had married Albert Calder in 1892.

Ellen O'Connor's *Memoir* was the only book about Myrtilla Miner, but several tributes were paid to her in print by her contemporaries. Harriet Beecher Stowe, in an article on "The Education of Freedmen," wrote in 1879: "In our national capital a brave, heroic woman, named Myrtilla Miner consecrated her life to founding a school for the young colored women of the District of Columbia, who had hitherto been left to ignorance and vice. Miss Miner wore out her own strength and shortened her life in this cause, but the school she founded still exists, and is doing a good work in Washington. In memory of her heroism the ladies' hall in Howard is called Miner Hall. Let her memory be blessed!"[15]

Senator Henry Wilson referred to Myrtilla Miner in a Senate debate as a "noble woman" and in his *History of the Rise and Fall of the Slave Power in America,* published in 1872, he wrote: "There is something touchingly impressive in the life and purpose of Miss Miner. In the great and grim tragedy of human affairs they afforded a delightful episode. In this selfish world, with its grasping and jostling throng she seemed like some angel ministrant on her mission of mercy. On the dark background of the nation's history it seemed an illuminated picture resplendent with truthfulness and love."[16]

Published tributes, however, cannot do justice to Myrtilla Miner's life and influence. It is the students of the Miner School, and *their* students in turn, whose lives and accomplishments attest the realization of her vision.

One of these, Miss Emma V. Brown, served as an assistant to Miss Emily Howland in 1858 when Miss Miner had to be away from the school because of ill health. She proudly wrote to Miss Miner: "Our school has increased considerably. We are literally packed. We have turned the kitchen into a primary school . . . We have had many visitors . . . among whom were a number of Quakers from England . . ."[17]

Miss Brown subsequently was graduated from Oberlin College[18] and later returned to Washington, to teach in the first school "for the colored race" in the District of Columbia.[19] Miss Emma Brown was but one of many Negroes who studied at the Miner School or at institutions helped by the Miner Fund.

It has been said that a teacher affects eternity. Who then can measure the extent of Myrtilla Miner's influence?

Florence B. Freedman
DEPARTMENT OF CURRICULUM & TEACHING
HUNTER COLLEGE OF THE CITY
UNIVERSITY OF NEW YORK

NOTES

[1] Wells, Lester Grosvenor, "Myrtilla Miner," *New York History,* Vol. 24, No. 3, p. 360.

[2] *Ibid.,* p. 362.

[3] O'Connor, Ellen M., *Myrtilla Miner: A Memoir,* pp. 16–17.

[4] *Ibid.,* pp. 23–25.

[5] Wells, *op. cit.,* p. 368.

[6] *Ibid.* M. M. to "Dear Friends," May 13, 1860, p. 370.

[7] Hatter, Henrietta R., *History of Miner Teachers College.* A Dissertation submitted to the Faculty of the Graduate School of Howard University, in partial fulfillment of the requirements of the degree of Master of Arts. Department of History. Washington, D.C., June, 1939 (unpublished), p. 13.

[8] Jean O'Connor to Grace Channing. Unpublished letter. Feinberg Collection.

[9] Library of Congress. (See *Manuscript Index of Library of Congress.*)

[10] Hatter, *op. cit.,* p. 43.

[11] The account of Ellen O'Connor's early life comes from an unpublished memoir by her sister, Mary Jane Tarr Channing, lent to me by her step-granddaughter, Mrs. Katharine Stetson Chamberlin of Pasadena, California. Ellen O'Connor's full story will be part

of a biography of William Douglas O'Connor that I am presently preparing.

[12] "Greenwood, Grace" (Sara Jane Clarke Lippincott), "An American Salon," *Cosmopolitan,* February, 1890, Vol. 8, pp. 437–447. Quotation on p. 445.

[13] Freedman, Florence B., "New Light on an Old Old Quarrel: Walt Whitman and William Douglas O'Connor, 1872," *Walt Whitman Review,* Vol. 11, No. 2, June, 1965, pp. 27–52.

[14] Calder, Ellen M., "Some Personal Reminiscences of Walt Whitman," *Atlantic Monthly,* Vol. 99, June, 1907, pp. 825 ff.

[15] Stowe, Harriet Beecher, "The Education of Freedmen," *North American Review,* Vol. 128, 1879, pp. 605–615. This quotation is on pp. 607–608. (It is interesting to note that in this article Myrtilla is spelled "Myrtella.")

[16] Wilson, Henry, *History of the Rise and Fall of the Slave Power in America* (3 vols.), Boston, 1871, Vol. 2, p. 582. (See Ellen O'Connor's *Memoir,* pp. 97–98.)

[17] Brown, Emma V. to M. M. April 11, 1858. Quoted in Wells, *op. cit.,* p. 369, n. 28.

[18] Oberlin College, leader in both co-education and Negro education, granted the first B.A. degree awarded to a Negro woman, Mary Jane Patterson, in 1862. At that time there were thirty-one Negro women and thirteen Negro men at Oberlin. (From the Special Report of the United States Commissioner of Educa-

tion, 1871, pp. 209–210. Quoted in Jeanne C. Noble, *The Negro Woman's College Education,* New York, Bureau of Publications, Teacher's College, Columbia University, 1956, p. 19. In this book, valuable as it is, it must be noted that Myrtilla Miner's name is spelled *Minor* and the date of the founding of the school is given as 1857 instead of 1851.)

[19] Wells, *op. cit.,* pp. 368–369.

MYRTILLA MINER

J.A.J Wilcox. Boston

Shine, gratefully,

Myrtilla Miner

MYRTILLA MINER

A Memoir

BOSTON AND NEW YORK
HOUGHTON, MIFFLIN AND COMPANY
The Riverside Press, Cambridge
1885

The Riverside Press, Cambridge:
Electrotyped and Printed by H. O. Houghton & Co.

To

THE PUPILS OF MYRTILLA MINER

AND

THE ALUMNI OF THE MINER NORMAL SCHOOL

𝕮𝖍𝖎𝖘 𝕸𝖊𝖒𝖔𝖎𝖗 𝖔𝖋 𝖙𝖍𝖊𝖎𝖗 𝕭𝖊𝖓𝖊𝖋𝖆𝖈𝖙𝖗𝖊𝖘𝖘

IS

AFFECTIONATELY INSCRIBED.

PREFACE.

THIS little volume is made up, as will be seen, of contributions from the friends of Miss Miner, giving such reminiscences as they could furnish; and from her own letters to various persons at different periods of her life ; also, from records in possession of the present Trustees of the Miner Fund. It is a source of disappointment that no letters have been found covering the period which she spent in Mississippi, as the experience of life in a slave State led to her coming to Washington to perform the work which these pages commemorate ; but all efforts to procure such letters, if any are extant, have been unavailing.

The thanks of the editor are due, and are gratefully expressed, to all who have in any manner aided in the preparation of this memoir.

Much regret is felt, that it is impossible, at this date, to name *all* who in those early days helped to sustain and encourage Miss Miner, whether by sums of money, or by sweet and needed sympathy.

ELLEN M. O'CONNOR.

WASHINGTON, D. C.,
November, 1885.

CONTENTS.

MEMOIR OF MYRTILLA MINER.

I.

Birth, Education, Preparation for her Work.

MYRTILLA MINER was born on the 4th of March, 1815, in Brookfield, Madison County, New York. Her father was a native of Norwich, Connecticut, and removed with his parents and brothers and sisters to Brookfield, when the country in which it is situated was little more than an unbroken wilderness. Here the family was subjected to all the privations incident to the lot of early settlers. They grew up strong men and women, with little education from schools, but with habits of industry and economy, which were transmitted to their children, accompanied by principles of high

moral integrity and deep religious rever-
ence.

Miss Miner's father was a man of uncommon natural ability, but, from his narrow
training, regarded mental culture, beyond
a certain limit, as superfluous and unnecessary. And so it was that his large family
were sent to school for a few years only,
acquiring readily the rudiments of an education ; but they could go no further.

Myrtilla was a bright child, of delicate
organization. She longed to study far beyond the limited range afforded by the
district school, and thus to fit herself for
something more congenial than the humble sphere of duties in the household and
on the farm. She borrowed books whenever she could do so. She read everything
that she could find, and profited by her
reading, yet her cravings were not satisfied.

Opportunities were rare in that remote
rural neighborhood for earning money,
and in the hop-picking season she eagerly
joined the ranks of the hop-pickers, that

she might earn a few dollars, to be spent
in books and other educational facilities.
Sometimes she did this when very weak
in body, since she was never strong, but
her indomitable will kept her up.   She
once earned seventeen dollars in this way,
when every basket she filled with the fra-
grant hops was attended with unutterable
weariness and pain; but so considerable
a sum could be earned by her in no other
way, and with it she might do so much to
further the object on the realization of
which her soul was fixed.

Determined to burst the bonds of cir-
cumstance which held her fast, she reached
out in many directions for help and counsel.   Once she wrote to Hon. William H.
Seward, then Governor of the State of New
York, asking him if he could show her
some way in which a girl in her circumstances might acquire a liberal education.

The Governor's reply, however, and perhaps inevitably and unavoidably, was vague
and unsatisfactory; as in those days the

rich endowments and other provisions for
the education of women which at present
ennoble and adorn the Empire State had
no existence.

So she struggled on. She began to teach
when fifteen years of age, and was an en-
thusiastic teacher, but, at the same time,
she deeply felt the need of being herself
taught. Soon she began to suffer from
spinal irritation, and was obliged to rest
from her labors as a teacher. In the mean
time she determined to go to school. She
applied to the principal of a school in Clinton, Oneida County, New York, for admis-
sion, for one year, on the condition that he
should wait for the payment of her board
and tuition until she should be able to earn
it by teaching. It was, indeed, pathetic to
see this young, frail girl, with her pale
face and lustrous eyes, pleading for an en-
trance to the halls of learning ; and perhaps it was the consciousness of this that
influenced Mr. B. to accept her conditions.
He saw that she had energy and determi-

nation, and decided to receive her on the terms she proposed. For a little time she forgot the symptoms heralding another attack of spinal suffering in the joy of being where the thirst for knowledge might be satisfied, and where she could breathe a more genial, social atmosphere.

But soon the dreaded disease again came upon her, and she was confined to her bed. The medical treatment of that time was of the heroic kind. Setons were inserted along the spine, with all the attendant physical agony; yet, through all her sufferings, this indomitable girl had her books brought to her, and learned the lessons for each day, thus keeping pace with the others in her class. As soon as well enough she was helped to the recitation-room, where, in a nearly recumbent position, she received the instruction of her teachers.

That the year in this school was of great advantage to her, even under all these adverse circumstances, may be inferred from the fact that she soon after received an appointment as teacher in one of the public schools of Rochester, New York, and soon was called to a similar position in Providence, Rhode Island, performing her duties acceptably to the board of trustees in each of those cities. Teaching was at that time the only field of employment open to a woman with her aspirations, and when a proposition was made to her to go to Mississippi for that purpose the offer was gladly accepted.

Now came a difficulty. She must have suitable clothing for the journey, and she had no money. She was a second time compelled to pledge her future earnings to obtain what was absolutely necessary for this purpose, and was all ready to leave for Mississippi when word came that the school would not open.

This left her in a very perplexing position, but she met the exigency with her customary courage and integrity. Having no immediate prospect of employment, she went to the merchants who had sold her goods on credit, and, telling her story, prevailed on them to take back every article that could be returned.

For a year after this she was without employment as a teacher, but, amid much discouragement, she plodded bravely along, and her good pluck was at last rewarded by another call from the South. This time she was not disappointed.

She went to Mississippi to teach in an institution for the education of planters' daughters, situated in Whitesville, Wilkinson County, and called the Newton Institute. This engagement brought her for the first time into actual contact with negro slavery.

When she so eagerly accepted the offer of a chance to earn an independent living in a milder climate and in a congenial field of labor, she had not dreamed of reform, nor of any philanthropic scheme whatever. But now the horrors of the slave system were suddenly revealed to her on the spot, through her own senses, by evidence that

could not be denied or concealed. The
sound of the lash was wafted to her ears in
the dim watches of the night. The slaves
herded and fed like beasts, steeped in sen-
suality, subjected to the unrestrained pas-
sions of brutal masters, — all this was
exposed to her view in its startling hideous-
ness. The effect of it upon this highly sensitive nature, with the moral and humane
sentiments so largely developed, may be
easily imagined. It determined her life-
work. She felt that she must do something to help destroy this monster. But
how to begin? At first, some Quixotic
plan to free the slaves at one blow was
conceived by her, and she corresponded
with an Anti-Slavery friend at the North
on the subject, but of course nothing
came of it.

Then her mind was directed to the idea
that the slaves must be educated. With
great boldness, as well as innocence, she
asked the planter, whose daughters she
was instructing, permission to teach the

slaves on his plantation, not knowing that it was a criminal offense, by the laws of Mississippi, to teach a slave to read. She was, of course, told that she could not be allowed to do this, and the legal reasons were explained to her. The planter added, also, the retort, "Why don't you go *North* and teach the 'niggers,' if you are so anxious to do it?" She then resolved that she *would* go North and teach them, and every day that purpose was strengthened.

Her stay in Mississippi lasted two years. During this time she protested against some of the cruelties of the slave system that came under her own observation, but of course only succeeded in having them removed farther from her reach. That, under these circumstances, she should have been retained so long in the South shows how much she was valued as a teacher. At last, the combined moral, mental, and physical strain was too much. Her health utterly gave way, and she was sent home, apparently to die. It was during this ill-

ness that she made a solemn pledge to
herself that if she recovered she would
devote the remainder of her life to the
elevation and welfare of the enslaved race.
This pledge she literally fulfilled, and now
it was that her true career opened unex-
pectedly before her. The outcome of all
her anxious thought upon the subject was,
at last, the determination to found a normal school for colored girls in the city of
Washington. This plan met the approval
of the friend to whom her former Quixotic
scheme had been confided, and she started
out to secure funds for its realization.

II.

Raising Funds to Start the School.

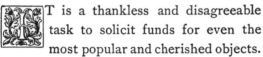T is a thankless and disagreeable task to solicit funds for even the most popular and cherished objects. We can imagine, then, the discouragements which must have beset the path of this woman as she pleaded in aid of a project to which a vast majority of her countrymen were bitterly hostile, and which many, if not most, of the friends of the slave regarded as foolhardy and useless. To attack the slave power on slave soil had come to be regarded as futile, as well as dangerous in the extreme. Garrison had tried the experiment in Baltimore, and it ended in an imprisonment, from which he was with difficulty extricated. Miss Miner's plan was, really, to sap the slave power by edu-

cating its victims, for the free blacks were crushed under its remorseless heel almost as much as if actually slaves themselves. So devoted a champion of his race as Frederick Douglass tells in the following letter to a trustee of the Miner School, with admirable candor, how he tried, in vain, to dissuade her from her undertaking : —

"You have often urged me to tell you the little (and it is but little) I remember of Miss Myrtilla Miner, the founder of what is now the Normal School for Colored Girls in the city of Washington. The task is, in every sense, an agreeable one.

"If we owe it to the generations that go before us, and to those which come after us, to make some record of the good deeds we have met with in our journey through life, and to perpetuate the memory and example of those who have in a signal manner made themselves serviceable to suffering humanity, we certainly should not forget the brave little woman who first in-

vaded the city of Washington, to establish
here a school for the education of a class
long despised and neglected.

"As I look back to the moral surroundings of the time and place when that school
was begun, and the state of public sentiment which then existed in the North as
well as in the South ; when I remember
how low the estimation in which colored
people were then held, how little sympathy
there was with any effort to dispel their
ignorance, diminish their hardships, alleviate their suffering, or soften their misfortunes, I marvel all the more at the thought,
the zeal, the faith, and the courage of
Myrtilla Miner in daring to be the pioneer
of such a movement for education here, in
the District of Columbia, the very citadel
of slavery, the place most zealously watched
and guarded by the slave power, and where
humane tendencies were most speedily detected and sternly opposed.

"It is now more than thirty years (but
such have been the changes wrought that

it seems a century) since Miss Miner, in company with Joseph and Phebe Hathaway (brother and sister), called upon me at my printing-office in Rochester, New York, and found me at work, busily mailing my paper, the ' North Star.' It was my custom to continue my work, no matter who came, and hence I barely looked up to give them welcome, supposing the call to be an ordinary one, perhaps of sympathy with my work, or, more likely, an act of mere curiosity, and continued. I was not long permitted, however, to treat my callers in this unceremonious way. I soon found I was in a presence that demanded my whole attention. A slender, wiry, pale (not over-healthy), but singularly animated figure was before me, and startled me with the announcement that she was then on her way to the city of Washington to establish a school for the education of colored girls. I stopped mailing my paper at once, and gave attention to what was said. I was amazed, and looked to see if the lady was in earnest and meant what she said.

"The doubt in my mind was transient. I saw at a glance that the fire of a real enthusiasm lighted her eyes, and the true martyr spirit flamed in her soul. My feelings were those of mingled joy and sadness. Here, I thought, is another enterprise, wild, dangerous, desperate, and impracticable, destined only to bring failure and suffering. Yet I was deeply moved with admiration by the heroic purpose of the delicate and fragile person who stood, or rather moved, to and fro before me, for she would not accept a chair.

" She seemed too full of her enterprise to think of her own ease, and hence kept in motion all the time she was in my office. Mr. and Miss Hathaway remained silent. Miss Miner and myself did the talking. She advocated the feasibility of her enterprise, and I (timid and faithless) opposed in all earnestness. She said she knew the South; she had lived among slave-holders; she had even taught slaves to read in Mississippi; and she was not afraid of violence in the District of Columbia. To me, the proposition was reckless, almost to the point of madness. In my fancy, I saw this fragile little woman harassed by the law, insulted in the street, a victim of slave-holding malice, and, possibly, beaten down by the mob. The fate of Prudence Crandall in Connecticut and the then recent case of Mrs. Douglass at Norfolk were before me; also my own experience in attempting to teach a Sunday-school in St. Michael's; and I dreaded the experience which, I feared, awaited Miss Miner.

" My argument made no impression upon the heroic spirit before me. Her resolution was taken, and was not to be shaken or changed.

" The result, I need not say, has justified her determination.

"I never pass by the Miner Normal School for Colored Girls in this city without a feeling of self-reproach that I could have said aught to quench the zeal, shake the faith, and quail the courage of the noble woman

by whom it was founded, and whose name
it bears.   Truly yours,
                    " FREDERICK DOUGLASS."
    WASHINGTON, *May* 4, 1883."

The following letter, written to a friend
in Smethport, Penn., about this time, indi-
cates how she was struggling to obtain the
means necessary to accomplish her mission.

                HAMILTON, N. Y., *February* 15, 1851.
    DEAR MRS. FORD, — . . . Let me say
to your good husband that I hardly think
I shall ever need any more certificates of
character or qualification, for I design
going to the city of Washington, to establish a school for the *colored children*, and I
can do this without any other certificate
than the one of *moral courage* I carry in
my own soul. Still, if they are able in
Smethport to give me something *extra*, in
the belief that I did exert an uncommon,
healthful influence upon their pupils, in-
tellectually, physically, and morally, I shall

cherish and be proud of it, whether I
should ever find occasion to use it or not.
In this proposed enterprise I should be
more glad of contributions than anything
else; for since I must go there a stranger,
I would gladly make my school *free* for a
single term, until I can convince them that
I am no humbug. . . .

M. MINER.

The lady, Mrs. Ednah Thomas, a member of the Society of Friends, to whom
Miss Miner had confided her former
scheme, wished her to wait until such a
sum of money could be raised as would
make the enterprise a safe venture. But
she answered, "I do not want the wealth
of Crœsus in my pocket to begin with;"
and so, with one hundred dollars, which
Mrs. Thomas provided, she undauntedly
began her life work. She begged from
her friends for the school, saying, "Give
me anything you have, — paper, books,
weights, measures, etc. I will make each

one an object lesson for my girls, explaining its source, its manufacture, uses, etc."

To-day, we can hardly imagine what such an undertaking as hers then was, when Washington was a stronghold of the pro-slavery element.

Some recollections of her at this time, from an early friend who was later a worker with her in the school, may be given here.

" I think," says the writer, " that I must have been about twenty years old when I first heard Myrtilla speak of this plan, or idea of hers, to go to Washington, to start a school for the free colored people of that city. I regarded the scheme as a very wild one, which might do for Myrtilla Miner, but scarcely for any one else in the world. Not so my mother. I have before me now Miss Miner's thin face, her penetrating eyes, her far-away look, as she came to my mother, very weary in body and very earnest in spirit, seeking some word of sympathy and encouragement in this proposed

undertaking. It seemed a great rest to
her spirit to find some one who was willing
to talk with her, and not oppose her project.   Under the influence of this kindly
sympathy, as she rested upon the lounge
in our dining-room, her whole frame seemed
to relax, and she looked younger and more
lovely than I ever remember to have seen
her, before or afterwards.

" She was grateful for my mother's
words of sympathy and cheer, and her great
resolution was renewed. She would go out
in the face of all opposition, — she would
go to Washington believing that she should
succeed. Her faith had triumphed over
her fears, and her soul was strengthened."

We next hear of her in Washington.

III.

Founding the School.

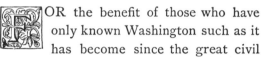OR the benefit of those who have only known Washington such as it has become since the great civil war, we will endeavor to sketch briefly the condition of society in that city, as it existed in 1851, in its relations to the colored people and the institution of slavery. Slavery was indeed the great dominant fact of the time, swaying everything before it, breaking up parties and churches alike, proving itself one of those burning questions that have no mercy for the repose of nations.

The compromise measures of 1850 had just been adopted, included in which was the infamous Fugitive Slave Law ; and no measure for the security of slavery ever

roused deeper indignation than the last-
named act. The slave power was extend-
ing its domain into the new lands of the
Southwest, and especially Texas, then recently acquired from Mexico. It was hunt-
ing its slaves throughout the free North,
and was regnant everywhere, — in the
church, in the state, in the press, in com-
merce, and in the college. Nothing was
exempt from its dominion. The abolitionists were a feeble band, like a voice crying
in the wilderness, demanding immediate
emancipation. The party formed for political action as yet had only dared to demand the restriction of slavery to the old
slave States, and its non-extension into the
territories of the United States then exist-
ing or that might be acquired. This party
was first known as the Liberty party, afterwards as the Free Democratic, and at
the time of which we write as the Free-
Soil party. The Republican party had
not yet been formed. There was a small
band of opponents of slavery in either

house of Congress, the most noted of
which, in the Senate, were Charles Sum-
ner, William H. Seward, Salmon P. Chase,
and John P. Hale; and in the House,
Joshua R. Giddings. These maintained
a gallant but almost hopeless struggle
against the slave oligarchy, which, in-
trenched in every department of the government, — executive, legislative, and judi-
cial, — felt its power to be secure, and was
already dreaming of new worlds to conquer.

The slaves in the District of Columbia
numbered several thousands. Their condition was not so deplorable as on the
cotton and sugar plantations, but some of
the most revolting features of the system
existed unconcealed. Gangs of slaves,
handcuffed together, to be sent for sale
further South, passed under the shadow of
the Capitol, and there was a slave pen,
with its whipping-post, across the river at
Alexandria. It was a crime to teach these
slaves to read the Sermon on the Mount.

In Washington, at this time, there were

also more than eight thousand free colored
people, not prohibited by any law from
obtaining a complete education, among
whom there might be two thousand children of suitable age to attend school. It
is hardly necessary to say that the vast
majority of the white population were bit-
terly opposed to their having any education whatever. The malignant and jealous
spirit of slavery which watched over the
national capital was not disposed to tolerate that anything but the merest rudiments
of learning should be dispensed to the free
people of color, so closely allied to the
slaves in blood and sympathy.

The class of free blacks was looked
upon by all supporters of the system of
slavery with peculiar suspicion and dislike.
It was a reproach to the master to feel
that there were some men and women, of
the same color and race as those he treated
like his cattle, who could walk the earth
and breathe the air of freedom on something like an equality with himself. To

the slave it was a dangerous example ; for behold, here was an African without an owner or master, which might lead him to think that a master or owner was not absolutely necessary in his own case. Several of the newer slave States, where the spirit of the system was most dominant and intolerant, had prohibited free colored people from remaining within their borders. But in the old slave States of Maryland and Virginia, from which the District of Columbia was originally formed, there was a considerable body of free colored people, the results of the manumission of slaves in former years, which, although sanctioned by the illustrious example of Washington, had long since ceased to be regarded with favor. The condition of this class, while of course immeasurably above that of a slave in some respects, was in others quite as bad or even worse. He could not testify in a court as a witness against a white man, much less sit on a jury, which latter act would have been

3

considered at that time as a ridiculous and impossible thing. He could not travel without a pass, and if found without one was immediately imprisoned. These disabilities made him particularly liable to outrage, for there was no one having even a proprietary interest in him to selfishly interpose in his behalf. Indeed, as Judge Taney said of the condition of the colored man at the time of the formation of the republic, "he had no rights which the white man was bound to respect." This meant that any crime might safely be committed upon his person or property ; and it was literally true of the free blacks, as a class, where they were fully exposed to the hatred and contempt of a slave-holding community. In Washington the condition of the free blacks was, however, mitigated to a certain extent by the fact that they were under the eye of many visitors from the North, members of Congress and others, who would report to the people at home any especially brutal treatment they might observe; and there was also a considerable infusion of Northern blood in the resident population. It should be mentioned here that about this time Dr. Gamaliel Bailey had succeeded, after a determined struggle, in establishing the "National Era" newspaper at the capital,— a Free-Soil newspaper on slave territory, — and around him gathered a limited circle of persons who held anti-slavery opinions. The tone of society, however, as a whole, was extremely Southern and pro-slavery.

It was into this community that Myrtilla Miner came with one hundred dollars in her hand with which to start a Normal School for Colored Girls, her main object being to fit young colored women to be teachers of their own race.

On December 3, 1851, the school was opened in a small apartment which had been hired for the purpose, with six pupils. The number increased to fifteen during the first month, and during the second to forty, which was the average for the first two

years, owing to the impossibility of securing larger rooms. Miss Miner, in one of
her appeals for aid, thus writes of the character of the schools for colored people ex-
isting in the city at the time she founded
hers : "There were previously five or six
private schools in the District, taught by
colored men, from which some of these
girls [referring to her pupils] professed to
have graduated, *i. e.*, learned all their instructors could teach them. But they were
unable to apply the knowledge they had
acquired to any practical use. While professing to be able to read well, they had no
proper understanding of what they read ;
while professing to understand grammar,
they rarely spoke or wrote good English ;
while professing to have advanced through
practical arithmetic, they could neither read
nor write numbers accurately, nor keep accounts with any correctness." "A little
learning is a dangerous thing," and pupils
like many of these who had been only half
taught, and, in some cases mis-taught, were

more difficult to train than those who had remained wholly uncultivated.

The letters which follow were written to a very dear friend in Smethport, Penn., and give a graphic account of her life in and for the school : —

WASHINGTON, *May* 17, 1852.

MY DEAR HANNAH, — ... More than two months have passed since I penned the preceding page with a right good will and a sure design of finishing this right speedily. I could not bear that one who truly loved me, as her works do show, that one whom I truly loved, as my works show not, should be longer left in doubt ; but my duties are oppressive. Since the weather has become warm I am obliged to allow myself more time for recreation. I wish I could lay a picture of all my doings and sayings before you since I commenced writing this. I wish I could have you by my side one week, while I rise early and toil late to accomplish well my work.

After seeking out and stimulating to
earnest exertion forty bright pupils for six
months, you should see me try to get aid to
build a schoolhouse for them ; you should
see all the letters I write for that purpose,
and then see all the people I am obliged to
call upon ; and then see me hunt out a nice
little colored girl, all untaught, to live with
the wife of a Congressman and be properly
brought up ; and see the many times I
walk a mile to accomplish this, besides
teaching five days in the week and doing
most of my sewing. I am already very
thin and pale, and have a walk of one mile
to school each day, besides all else. It is
true I ride home in the omnibus at three
o'clock, because it is oppressively warm,
and I have no dinner until after school,
which makes me faint as well as weary.

I could not secure a good boarding place
near my school, for that is nearly out of
town, the people having obliged us to move
twice to get out of their way, and now per-
mitting us to have no better school-room

than a private dwelling affords, and that very small. Many ladies refused to take me to board because I would teach colored girls, and much else of obloquy and contempt have I endured because I would be about my Master's business. I heed it not, though I am to-night informed that the new mayor will abolish all colored schools. I care not.

If God hath not sent me to this work, I hope he will raise up means to defeat me in all my purposes ; and if it is his work, and he has permitted me to be the instrument of its commencement, no man or men can frustrate the design, and all their efforts will prove unavailing. I cannot half answer your two good full letters, but I wish you to write me again, and I will try to answer some time, though it may be months first ; for I have constantly a vast number of business letters and letters of inquiry on hand to answer, and can usually keep up with all that is absolutely necessary.

I was delighted to receive the letters from the little maidens, and will enclose a note for them all together, and not only for those who wrote, but all the rest that love and wish to hear from me. I am interested in all you write, especially in the teacher now at college, etc. . . . Love to all, and in truth thine, M. MINER.

The following letter to the same friend, of a later date than the foregoing, exhibits her devotion to her work and the pleasure she took in it : —

WASHINGTON, *October* 20, 1852.

MY FRIEND BELOVED, — I must begin anew. Far away from *here* was I, at the commencement of this sheet, and a world-full have I seemed to live since then. You will forgive the delay when I tell you that I labored continually, during my vacation, to secure *funds*, hoping to purchase *a place* for my school ; that at one time I deemed it entirely certain, but one hour's delay on the part of the agent here allowed it to be sold beyond our reach. This nearly distracted me with disappointment, so that I could not write to any one, and therefore my Providence visit passed almost in silence, aside from constant exertions, which after all have brought us no immediate relief. I have returned to open school in the same little rooms, which are crowded with the thirty-three already entered, and a throng is yet in reserve for the winter.

I love this school of mine profoundly, and have really no idea, when I am with them, that they are not white, recognizing their *spiritual* more than their physical. Some, indeed many, *spirits* with whom I come in contact here seem far darker than they.

I have never before felt myself exactly in my own "*niche*," fully satisfied with the work I had to do ; because I never before realized all the benefits resulting to the world from my labors that I hope are embodied here.

Feeling full content in obscurity, caring not that the *vain world* comprehend my motives, so that such loved ones as *you* appreciate them, I rest in peace. . . .

I was *sick* when your letter came, scarcely able to be about, yet in my school until the middle of July ; since then, every moment busy. . . . I hope to have a permanent place for myself and school before the year is past, and if your friends the "Kings," or any others, can be induced to contribute aid, grant us your influence, for property is so high we shall be obliged to pay about one thousand dollars to secure one appropriate.

With kind regards to all the dear friends, believe me devotedly yours, in *prayer* that good angels may guard you and yours ever more.   MYRTLE MINER.

The following are extracts from a letter written in the spring of 1853 : —

"My thirty-eighth birthday has gone by,

and that, too, rather sadly. It was the day of Pierce's inauguration, — noisy, boisterous, stormy, and fatiguing, just as I never wish a birthday to be. I always count these as *way-marks*, or points for erecting altars, where the heart's incense may rise, acknowledging all the good of the past, and throwing into the censer the great hopes of the future. I know of no more effectual mode of dissolving *grief* than this noting the way-marks, dotting the whole way of life with thanksgiving, and especially wherever we see mercy interfering with our short-sighted plans, and solving the mystery of greater good.

"Another mode is that of scanning the inner temple, to learn just how much of sorrow comes from the disappointment of our favorite plans, drawn often in selfish pride, or ambition altogether earthly, and frequently of such a character that, if consummated, we must be swallowed in the depths of the moral quagmire they produce. . . .

"It is a hard thing I have here attempted, and I often fear I have not the strength necessary to perform well the part assigned; but if I can prepare the way for some *nobler spirit,* my duty will be done. . . .

"I hold myself to this work, for we have now bought a whole city square of ground for the school, more than three acres, at a cost of four thousand dollars, and the funds are to be raised to pay for it and build soon.

". . . I forgot to tell you that I think God designs to employ the feminine principle more in this age for the redemption of the world; therefore, Clara must not be worshipped, but trained to strength and fitted for great action. . . .

"Ever yours in living faith,

"MYRTLE MINER."

The following letter, written in the autumn of 1853, fully shows the condition of the school at that period: —

"I am so glad you questioned particularly about our school, for I say *our* to everybody that helps. It reminds me that I am in the habit of thinking *all* my friends must be familiar with facts which I have written to a few ; but, surely, I thought I acknowledged the receipt of the five dollars enclosed in your Wisconsin letter, for it was *that letter* I last answered.

"I did receive it ; it came most opportunely, at a time when I was sore pressed for want of funds, for those times do frequently come. I had just returned from my summer travels, 'out of pocket,' as usual, and waited four long weeks in suspense, with current expenses going on, hoping to get possession of our own purchased property to open my school. The scholars were all impatient and anxious, and twice, meanwhile, came out with their satchels of books to find the school ; and at last I was obliged to rent a place to open school, our own having to pass through the process of an arbitration between the tenant and landlord who sold it to us, before we can be permanently settled. This purchased place, of which we have the *deed* (and only wait temporarily for possession), cost four thousand dollars. It is a whole square of ground, comprising more than three acres, a little out of town, in a thriving neighborhood, convenient to market, etc. Has on it a small frame house and barn, many fruit and shade trees, etc. It is held by two men in Philadelphia, who accepted and gave security for the two thousand dollars loaned, spoken of in the circular, thus becoming self-constituted trustees. All moneys contributed for the purchase are paid over to them immediately, I not reserving sufficient to pay my travelling expenses. . . . Mrs. Stowe has sent us one thousand dollars of the 'Uncle Tom's Cabin' money, and several other individuals have contributed each one hundred dollars, others fifty dollars, — among these, Dr. Bailey of the 'Era;' and, of course, these people must be well assured

of the profitable and right appropriation
of these funds, which is the best assurance
I can give your Smethport friends in so
short a letter.

"Dr. Bailey has always been ready to
publish anything for the school (which has
been successfully sustained two years next
December) in the 'Era,' and has often
requested it ; but, when acquainted with
the local objections, until our place was
purchased, has thought best to refrain ;
but you will have something soon, and
also a full first annual report, giving the
rise, progress, and present state, which is
indeed most encouraging.

"When the school did open this month,
the pupils rushed in so happy in the appreciation of the blessing, so hearty in study,
so neat in appearance, and so quiet in
manners, that I have experienced only joy
in teaching them.

"We were in a new place, it being the
fourth the school has occupied since its
establishment, and as usual there were some

threats about breaking it up ; but, when
the pupils assembled, all mutineers seemed
struck dumb with its beautiful appearance,
and no one has done the least thing to
disturb us. On the contrary, the old man
who rented me the rooms said, ' Why, I
never see nicer looking scholars in my life ;
nobody will disturb these ! and then they
are the quietest set I ever see. You would
not know there was a school in the house,
to come into the hall, unless the door was
opened in the schoolroom.'   All this is
true, and yet we have two large rooms,
one above and one below, not as convenient as we could wish, nor can we expect
to secure such until we build.   Two thousand dollars are already contributed for
our place, and two thousand loaned, so that
it is paid for ; but we have yet to meet the
loan, and then build as good a house as
we can afford.   The school books and also
a small library have been contributed by
publishers and friends, but the teacher's
support (I have an assistant) comes from

such of the pupils as are able to pay one dollar and fifty cents a month, and have everything found them. This would be a fair support in Smethport, with an average of forty pupils, twenty-five of whom pay regularly, but here, where board is twenty dollars per month, it is a mere pittance. If your friend, Mr. Allen, will write me, I will gladly give any further intelligence in my power ; or, if there are still any questions unanswered for you, remind me, and they shall be promptly attended to. The reason we have published so little, while the school was prospering to the delight of all who saw it, was to avoid the possibility of defeat in our plans to purchase such a place as we pleased ; but now that is over, you will hear enough from us, I presume.

"Remember me kindly to all the dear ones, and believe me, in truth,

"Ever the same,

"M. Miner."

4

WASHINGTON, *May* 3, 1854.

BELOVED, — . . . You know my hours are
not my own ; they scarcely were in the
life I lived with you ; much less now.   If
only my school duties rested on me I could
strongly bear them, but since the 1st of
March, when I became thirty-nine years
old, I have had housekeeping cares, for
then we got possession of our own pleasant
school and home ; and as the " Edmondson
family " [1] resided fourteen miles out in the
country, and must have time to move here,
Emily and I had to do our own cooking
and all for a month.   But now that is past,
and we have three little people boarding
with us, to watch over, wash, dress, and
comprehend, — the last the hardest of all.
For a few weeks after we moved to this
place, which was in a most forlorn and
desolate condition, with no fence to bound
its broad acres and thrifty fruit trees, no
security to its old clattering houses, the

---

[1] A family of colored people who came to live on the place.
Emily, the daughter, assisted in the school.

locks and bolts, blinds and fastenings,
seeming to have had a general rebellion
and "stepped out," Emily and I lived here
alone, unprotected, except by God, the
rowdies occasionally stoning our house at
evening, and we nightly retiring in the
expectation that the house would be fired
before morning. Why it was not can only
be referred to the fact that He who permits the wrath of man to praise Him re-
straineth the remainder. On one occasion,
while the stones were falling upon the
house weightily, I rushed out and walked
a whole square to get a man to go for the
night watch, and in about fifteen minutes
four very savage-looking men, armed with
clubs, etc., made their appearance, giving
the kind assurance that they would keep
an eye to our safety. Since then our high,
hard - to - get - over picket fence has been
built, Emily and I have been seen practicing shooting with a pistol, the family have
come, and a dog with them, and we have
been left in most profound peace. We

have many good trees, some shrubs, rasp-
berries, strawberries, rhubarb, and aspara-
gus in abundance, the place having once
been cultivated for fruit and vegetables,
and many remnants being left.   All this is
very agreeable, but it gives me care, and
makes me work, and taxes my invention
to direct others.   These things devolve
upon me because the trustees reside in
Philadelphia, and cannot come to attend to
them.   The consequence is that with forty-
five pupils I have enough to do to keep
me fully alive. . . .

My school has been visited to-day by
people from Kentucky, New Hampshire,
Massachusetts, Canada, and Washington.
. . . With love to all thine and others,

Ever thy   MYRTLE.

WASHINGTON, *November* 8, 1854.

MY DEAR FRIEND, — Late at night and
weary, but just recovering from an attack
of chills and fever, which came of dreadful,
dreadful weariness, I seize my pen hastily

to tell you how sorely I have been pressed by care, and therefore you, with all my dear friends, have been left unnotified of my fate.

But Cleopha's little letter will show you how early I designed giving you some knowledge of our safe return. When I reached home I found Emily, on whom I depended for help, just ready to start North to collect funds to buy her brother, who is a slave ; and behold, I was left with three little boarders to watch over out of school, thirty-five scholars to teach during the day, and all my fall work, fitting up this old house for winter ; and it being our first winter in it, it was no small task to bring things into Yankee comfort. . . . This is why you have not heard from and received all the kind expressions due yourself and the Smethport friends. The children [1] and I talk much of our visit there, and they have repeated to their schoolmates all that occurred, even to the play-

---

[1] Colored children who were cared for in the writer's family.

ing hide-and-seek, and getting up in their night-gowns, etc. . . .

Oh, how glad I am for the long, quiet, resting visit I had with you!

Everywhere else they kept me stirring, and sometimes I wearied sadly. But, upon the whole, I was glad I took the children, for when they returned and stood by their schoolmates I saw that they had improved astonishingly. We had some amusing scenes, I assure you. At one place the people had a big meeting, made the children sing their little songs alone in church, and then took up a collection of more than twenty dollars.

My school prospers in spite of my weakness, and I must bid you adieu and rest. Remember me to thy good husband. In love to thee and all,   Myrtle.

IV.

The Pro-Slavery Opposition to the School.

FROM the earliest development of her plan to teach colored girls in Washington, Miss Miner had to encounter the hostility of the community in general, although it did not reach the point of a formal protest from the leading elements of society until the school had been in progress for a number of years.

What she had most to fear from the beginning was rowdyism and incendiarism. She prepared to meet the former by practicing with a pistol, and training herself to take good aim by shooting at a mark. One of the most annoying manifestations was that of rowdies congregating near her school to insult the girls as they came out on their way home. One of her pupils of this time says, "She was one of the brav-

est women I have ever known ; and just
here I am reminded of an incident which
occurred one night while I was with her,
when the evening school was in session.
Some rowdies came to the school-house.
She stood bravely at the window with a
revolver, and declared she would shoot the
first man who came to the door.   They re-
treated at once."   Once her house was set
on fire, but a passer-by awoke her, and
helped to put it out.   Stones were frequently thrown at her windows in the
night-time, and she was otherwise annoyed.
It is related that at one time, in answer to
threats of violence, she fearlessly and in-
dignantly exclaimed, "Mob my school!
You dare not! If you tear it down over
my head I shall get another house.   There
is no law to prevent my teaching these
people, and I shall teach them, even unto
death!"   Looking into her earnest face
and flashing brown eyes they saw that she
would do it.

It is interesting to learn that the President's carriage came often to the humble school door to bring Mrs. Means, an aunt of Mrs. Pierce, who was attracted by Miss Miner's enthusiasm. Such countenance from so high a source probably did much to hold in check the hatred of the mob, which was at times threatening and troublesome.

It was the custom of Miss Miner to issue circulars, almost annually, appealing for aid in carrying on her enterprise. Some time previous to 1856 the funds and property of the school were placed under the care of a board of trustees, of which Rev. W. H. Beecher, then of Reading, Massachusetts (a brother of Rev. Henry Ward Beecher), was secretary. Mr. Beecher issued a circular in December, 1856, in behalf of the school, which seems to have attracted much attention. In fact, it stirred up a spirit of opposition in Washington which appeared likely to terminate seriously, and for a time Miss Miner, who was then absent, was in doubt whether her presence in Washington would not create active disturbance.

The most important article that appeared in opposition to the school was written by Mr. Walter Lenox, at one time mayor of the city of Washington. It was evidently carefully considered, and was printed in the "National Intelligencer" of May 6, 1857. It is reproduced here in full, as a very significant document, historically considered, showing the high tide which pro-slavery feeling had reached, when one of the most conservative and respectable of American newspapers could open its columns for such an attack on one feeble woman for teaching a few innocent girls to read and write the language of Algernon Sidney and Patrick Henry.

To the Editors. — Entertaining the opinion that the following article, taken from the "Boston Journal," should be made known to the citizens of this District, I request its republication, with the accompanying comments, in your paper.

Walter Lenox.

From the " Boston Journal" of April 18, 1857.

SCHOOL FOR FREE COLORED GIRLS IN WASHINGTON. — There are in the United States five hundred thousand free people of color. They are generally, although subject to taxation, excluded by law or prejudice from schools of every grade. Their case becomes at once an object of charity, which rises infinitely above all party or sectional lines. This charity we are gratified in being able to state has already been inaugurated, through the devoted labors of an excellent young lady from Western New York, by the name of Miss Myrtilla Miner, who has established and maintained for the past four years in the city of Washington a school for the education of free colored youth. This school is placed there because it is national ground, and the nation is responsible for the well-being of its population; because there are there eleven thousand of this suffering people excluded by law from schools and destitute of instruction;

because there are in the adjoining States
of Maryland and Virginia one hundred
and thirty thousand equally destitute, who
can be reached in no other way; and because it is hoped through this means to
reach a class of girls of peculiar interest,
often the most beautiful and intelligent,
and yet the most hopelessly wretched, and
who are often objects of strong paternal
affection. The slaveholder would gladly
educate and save these children, but domestic peace drives them from his hearth;
he cannot emancipate them to be victims
of violence or lust; he cannot send them
to Northern schools, where prejudice
would brand them; and it is proposed to
open an asylum near them, where they may
be brought, emancipated, educated, and
taught housewifery as well as science, and
thus be prepared to become teachers among
their own mixed race.

In its present condition this school embraces boarding, domestic economy, normal
teachers, and primary departments, and is

placed under the care of an association, consisting of the following trustees : Benjamin Tatham, New York ; Samuel M. Janney, Loudoun County, Virginia ; Johns Hopkins, Baltimore ; Samuel Rhoads and Thomas Williamson, Philadelphia ; G. Bailey and L. D. Gale, Washington ; H. W. Bellows, New York ; C. E. Stowe, Andover ; H. W. Beecher, Brooklyn ; together with an executive committee consisting of S. J. Bowen, J. M. Wilson, and L. D. Gale, of Washington ; and M. Miner, principal, and Wiliam H. Beecher, of Reading, secretary.

The trustees state that a very eligible site of three acres, within the city limits of Washington, of the northwest, has already been purchased, paid for, and secured to the trustees, and that all which is now wanted is $20,000 wherewith to erect a larger and more suitable edifice for the reception of the applicants pressing upon it from the numerous free colored blacks in the District and adjacent States. The proposed edifice is designed to accommodate one hundred and fifty scholars, and to furnish homes for the teachers, and pupils from a distance. The enlarged school will include the higher branches in its system of instruction.

There was a meeting yesterday afternoon, in an anteroom of Tremont Temple, of gentlemen called together to listen to the statements of the secretary of the Association regarding this school. The meeting was small, but embraced such gentlemen as Hon. George S. Hillard, Rev. Dr. Lothrop, Rev. E. E. Hale, and Deacon Greele, all of whom are deeply interested in the project.

The meeting decided to draw up and circulate a subscription paper, and counted upon receiving $10,000 for the purpose in this city. The pastors of several churches in New York have pledged their churches in the sum of a thousand dollars each. Mr. Beecher will solicit subscriptions in most of the principal towns of Massachu-

setts. The designs and benefits of the project will be fully set forth at a public meeting in this city in the course of a fortnight.

It is not my purpose to notice the impu-
tations which the above extract contains,
or my desire to provoke a sectional controversy. The matter involved is too mo-
mentous in all its relations, not only to this
community, but to the entire country ; and,
in the language of the extract itself, " rises
infinitely above all party or sectional lines."
It is my wish to arrest public attention here,
as also elsewhere, in order that such immediate measures may be adopted as the
exigency of the case demands. If I do not
entirely mistake the opinion which the citizens of this District will entertain of the
character and fatal consequences of this
enterprise, they will almost universally,
without distinction of party or class, emphatically protest against it, and will con-
fidently expect that the advocates of this
measure will promptly abandon it, as an

unjust and dangerous interference with the
interests and feelings of a separate independent community.

The proposition is to establish at the
city of Washington, upon an extensive
scale, an academy for the education of free
colored males and females from every section of the Union. Let us calmly view the
question both in its local and national as-
pects. The District of Columbia contains
about three thousand six hundred slaves
and ten thousand free colored persons.
This latter class embraces very many most
worthy members, who contribute to the
wealth of the community, but the necessi-
ties of a large portion of them impose an
onerous tax upon the public revenue and
upon private charity. This condition of
things does not arise exclusively from
their own demerits : they have been grad-
ually and to a very considerable extent
ousted by the increase of white labor from
the positions formerly filled by them as
domestics and laborers. Their number,

originally too large in proportion to our white population, is increasing rapidly both by their natural increase and from immigration. Justice to ourselves and kindness to them require that we should prohibit immigration and encourage their removal from our limits. Now, it is plainly manifest that the success of this school enterprise must largely increase our negro population by the inducements it offers. The schools will be increased with the demand. It will bring not only scholars to remain temporarily, but entire families, until our District is inundated with them. Upon white labor, upon the present colored residents of the District and their descendants, and upon the public generally, this increase must operate most injuriously. If, however, we should admit that the increase from this cause would be trifling, and that the instruction would be mainly confined to our own resident population, the following insuperable objection presents itself : —

The standard of education which is proposed is far beyond the primary branches,
and will doubtless from time to time be advanced.   Is it, then, just to ourselves, or
humane to the colored population, for us to
permit a degree of instruction so far beyond their political and social condition,
and which must continue to exist in this
as in every other slaveholding community?
With this superior education there will
come no removal of the present disabilities,
no new sources of employment equal to
their mental culture ; and hence there will
be a restless population, less disposed than
ever to fill that position in society which is
allotted to them.   In my judgment, these
two objections — the increase of our free
population and the indiscriminate education of them far beyond their fixed condition — are sufficient reasons for us to
oppose this scheme.

But let us consider the subject in its
more important relations to the whole
country.   There has been for many years

a persistent agitation of the question of the abolition of slavery in this District. It is one of the leading purposes of a powerful, if not controlling section of the Republican party. The advocates of this measure know that it is hopeless to attempt the accomplishment of it, through the legislation of the national government, without the consent of all parties interested, and therefore they deem it necessary to adopt an indirect course. Again, although the Constitution prohibits any interference with slavery in the States, yet its abolition is the determined resolve of a large portion of the Republican party, highly distinguished for talents and energy. For this purpose they hold themselves justified in using every influence within their reach. Without charging this intent upon all the authors and present supporters of this enterprise, can we doubt, in view of the past history and present action of " abolitionism," that this institution will be controlled by it, and employed at an early day with-

out disguise for these purposes ?   We cannot be unmindful of the character and aims
of some of those announced as its principal
advocates ; and even if this particular one
should be preserved from such influences,
yet, under the precedent it would afford,
others would   be established for these
special objects.

A misguided philanthropy, inflamed by
political demagogism, would readily supply
the means and the agents to execute its
designs ; an incendiary press in our midst
will soon follow, and, with all these varied
and active agencies, stimulated by the
presence of adherents in Congress, in constant operation, our District will be con-
verted into the headquarters of " slavery
agitation," from which it may deal forth in
every direction its treasonable blows.   It
is unnecessary to depict the fatal consequences to ourselves and to the country ;
but, in considering this view of the subject,
we cannot forget the events which disturbed the peace of our country some few

years since, consequent upon the act of
Drayton and Sayres ; and how quickly the
agitation attendant upon it spread from the
crowded streets and excited populace to the
halls of Congress. If these apprehensions,
then, are not altogether unfounded, either
in their relation to ourselves or the country
generally, we must meet the responsibilities
they impose. We shall gain nothing by
concession or delay. This scheme was
started some years ago in humble guise,
and in the foothold it has already gained it
feels secure of its future progress. Earnest, prompt action can now arrest it peace-
fully ; tumult and blood may stain its future history.

With justice we can say to the advocates
of this measure, you are not competent
to decide this question ; your habits of
thought, your ignorance of our true relations to the colored population, prevent
you from making a full and candid examination of its merits, and, above all, the tem-
per of the public mind is inauspicious even

for its consideration. If your humanity
demands this particular sphere for its action, and if, to use your own language,
prejudice would brand them at your Northern schools, establish separate institutions
in the free States, dispense your money
there abundantly as your charity will supply, draw to them the unfortunate at your
own door, or from abroad, and in all respects gratify the largest impulses of your
philanthropy ; but do not seek to impose
upon us a system contrary to our wishes
and interests, and for the further reason
that by so doing you injure the cause of
those whom you express a wish to serve.
We must insist that within our limits we
are the best, and must be the exclusive,
judges of the character and degree of
instruction that shall be imparted to this
class of our population ; who shall be their
teachers, and what the nature of the influences they may seek or shall be permitted
to exercise. We have not been insensible
heretofore to their wants, and still hold our-

selves ready to minister to them with all proper liberality and with far better judgment than strangers. We fully acknowledge and respect our relations to the general government and to the citizens of the States, but in this matter we alone must be the conservators of our own peace and welfare. And, still further, we cannot tolerate an influence in our midst which will not only constantly disturb the repose and prosperity of our own community and of the country, but may even rend asunder the " Union itself." Such a protest it is the duty of our corporate authorities to make. Its beneficent effect may be to persuade the supporters of this scheme to abandon its further prosecution; but if otherwise, the responsibility will be with those who by their own wanton acts of aggression make resistance a necessity and submission an impossibility.   W. L.

It is difficult to characterize the foregoing letter as it deserves, at the present time, when African slavery with all its abominations has been swept away ; but it is worth dwelling on for a moment as revealing the baleful influence which that institution exerted over the minds of men otherwise upright and honorable.

Mr. Lenox's objections can be summed up under four heads : (1) The school would attract free colored people from the adjoining States ; (2) That it was proposed to give them an education far beyond what their political and social condition would justify ; (3) That the school would be a centre of influence directed against the existence of slavery in the District of Columbia ; (4) That it might endanger the institution of slavery, and even rend asunder the Union itself !

Further, as worthy of special notice, attention is called to the arrogant assumption of the right to be "the exclusive judges of the character and degree of instruction that shall be imparted to the class of free colored people," which this gentleman makes, speaking on behalf of the rulers of Washington society of that date ; and finally, the covert justification of mob violence in case "the protest of the corporate authorities should be unavailing," with which the article closes.

The object of this attack was a Christian woman seeking, with a zeal and self-devotion worthy of the early Christian martyrs, to elevate and bless with knowledge, refinement, and virtue some hapless maidens "guilty only of a skin not colored like our own."

It will seem incredible to future generations that the author of this article was esteemed to be a Christian gentleman ; that he spoke the sentiments of an overwhelming majority of the refined society of which he was a member ; and that he wrote it in the middle of the nineteenth century, in the capital city of the great republic, whose boast then was that it was the freest government on the globe.

As the proper addendum to this article

and resulting from it, we give below from
the pen of her associate an account of an
interview which, in the autumn of 1857,
Miss Miner sought with Mr. Seaton, of the
famous firm of Gales and Seaton, editors
of the "National Intelligencer."

The writer with some trepidation accompanied Miss Miner to the office of the
"National Intelligencer." Upon being ush-
ered into the dignified presence of the editor Miss Miner asked Mr. Seaton, "Can
you spare me a moment's conversation?"
He replied: "Certainly."

Miss M. Some time in last May an
article appeared in the "National Intelligencer" concerning my school. I wish
to know if you were aware of its import.

Mr. Seaton. I was. It was written with
my consent and under my advisement.
After the appearance of a circular propos-
ing the erection of a large institution for
educating negroes in this city, Mr. Lenox
called and asked what I thought of his

writing an article opposing it. I concurred in its being done and printed. I have no objection to your school nor to educating the negroes, but I do object strongly to having them collected here in numbers for any purpose whatever, and that seemed the intention distinctly stated in the plan for the proposed academy, or whatever it was to be.

An invitation was extended to all throughout the Union, no limit. We have enough of them and more than enough. They are crowding our jails and poorhouses, being shut out of most employments.

I have always favored their education, and would do as much for it as for the education of the white race. When mayor I attended Mr. Cook's public examination, and protected them from rowdies. My sole aim in this article was against having them gathered here from a distance, making this a great centre, which would be the effect of the school you proposed.

The negroes have now quite a strong
tendency here in consequence of no law
being in force against their coming.

Those now living here are, and have
always been, provided with schools. There
are six schools here taught by teachers of
their own color. [In reply to Miss Miner
he said :] I think I have stated Mr. Lenox's
view also. He might have had political
motives, but I think not.

Miss M. But he referred to politics.
He alluded to the Republican party, and
the article has been the means of remov-
ing Dr. Gale [1] from the Patent Office.

Mr. S. That is a very far-fetched idea.
It is begging the question. I know no
more of Dr. Gale than of the Apostle Paul.
It is not probable that the President knew
anything about the article, but he has been
told by some one who wished Dr. Gale's
removal that he was an abolitionist or a

[1] Dr. L. D. Gale had accepted a place on the board of trustees of
Miss Miner's school; hence the supposition. The pleasant home
of the "ever-blessed Gales," as she styled them, was one of Miss
Miner's resting places, where she was always welcome.

Free Soiler. You know in this boasted land of liberty there is no freedom. It may cost a man his bread to have opinions of his own. He must go to France or Russia for freedom ; there is none here.

There was no intention on my part to refer to any party. Personalities are not admitted to the columns of the "Intelligencer." If anything of the kind comes to my knowledge it is stricken out. We have not for thirty years admitted any discussions of slavery into our columns, except, of course congressional debates.

Surrounded by danger, at any time a mob, armed with bludgeons and pistols, may fill our streets. The agitation of the subject does no good, but great harm. We must trust to Providence to remove this anomalous system in his own time; we can do nothing.

The "Higher Law" men would smile at mobs, bloodshed, anything caused by doing what they thought right. I prefer peace. I can understand how Northern men must feel strongly on this subject, how odious it must seem to them. It is a great abstract wrong. I should think it a great wrong to enslave a man, but when he is already a slave I should not hesitate to retain him in that condition. Once more, this and this only is the ground of opposition to your school [repeating what he had before stated], but I see not why you did not go to the writer of the article in question instead of coming here.

Miss M. Because it derived all its power from the fact of its being printed in the "Intelligencer," not any from the writer. Have you seen Dr. Bailey's review of it in the "Era"? That gives statistics showing that the colored population of this city has not for several years increased in the same ratio as the white, nor in the same proportion as in former years, and the diffusion of education and intelligence would certainly further this diminution. At least, education makes them safer inhabitants.

Mr. S. I have not seen the "Era" more than twice within the year. I was much opposed to its establishment here as tending to cause bad feeling. No doubt the article in question is able. I have a great respect for Dr. Bailey. I know there is nothing to be feared from these people when educated ; they are a docile race, but Africa is the place for them.

Miss M. They will go there when they become intelligent enough to understand their true interest.

Mr. S. I think not. It is only the slaves manumitted with that purpose in view who will go ; the free negroes will not leave this country.

Miss M. The idea of trying to elevate this people was first presented to my mind from seeing the degrading influence slavery exerted on the white race.

Mr. S. Yes. It will be but a drop in the Pacific Ocean.

V.

History of the School.

AS has already been stated, the school was founded in December, 1851, and soon attained an average attendance of about forty pupils, composed of young girls, chiefly from the more well-to-do colored families of the city.

Miss Miner seems to have issued a printed circular nearly every year, as before stated, appealing to the benevolent for aid in her enterprise, and her summer vacations were devoted to traveling in the North and making personal appeals for the same object. She very early became aware of the necessity of securing a permanent location for the school. In one of her early circulars she says, "The greatest obstacle to be met was that of securing suitable rooms, arising from the well-known prejudice against letting respectable premises for such a purpose. Owing, chiefly, to this cause, the school has already been subjected to several removals. Having surmounted many obstacles, and outlived, in some measure, the prejudice which at one time threatened to crush the attempt to educate the defenseless, it is most desirable that a permanent situation be secured."

In 1853, a lot had been purchased in the city of Washington, comprising about three acres, with two small frame-houses upon it, situated between 19th and 20th Streets, and N Street and New Hampshire Avenue, being described on the plan of the City as Square No. 115. The cost of this property was about $4,300. It was purchased and held in trust for the purposes of the school by Thomas Williamson and Samuel Rhoads, two benevolent members of the Society of Friends residing in Philadelphia. (Mr. Williamson was the father of Passmore Williamson, who was impris-

6

oned for aiding in the escape of slaves.)
Towards the payment for the property the
trustees had, up to January 1, 1854, received about $2,500, and the remainder was
unpaid.   On the 1st of March, 1854, after
much trouble in dislodging the former ten-
ants, the school was finally established on
its own property, and one of the houses
on the lot became the home of Miss Miner,
as well as of the school.

The remoteness of the location from the
settled part of the city had its disadvan-
tages, as she was often alone at night, with
only an assistant teacher, who lived with
her, and was consequently exposed to the
attacks of rowdies, and worse, who were
disposed to do her and her school harm.
But still it was a great point gained to
have the school stand upon its own ground
with room for indefinite expansion.   And,
through all the hate and pro-slavery prejudice, the school lived and thrived.   Friends
rallied to aid and make it permanent.
Members of the Society of Friends in

Philadelphia and other places gave largely to its founder. Among these Thomas Williamson, Samuel Rhoads, Benjamin Tatham, Jasper Cope, and Catherine Morris were liberal donors. Mrs. Harriet Beecher Stowe gave $1,000, as well as hearty sympathy and support to the work. So that by the year 1856 the property purchased for the school had been fully paid for. Her valued assistant teacher, whom we have before quoted, gives us a brief glimpse of Miss Miner's labors during these years, which may be inserted here :

"How she worked and talked to arouse colored people to see the importance of what she wished to do ; how, out of school hours, she begged money of members of Congress and Senators, and importuned writers for the press to visit and report facts relative to her work; or how she spent her vacations interesting the benevolent, getting their aid; or in gathering the library of several hundred volumes ; or obtaining the current literary magazines and periodicals to improve and enlighten, can never be fully told."

All this shows what one energetic woman, alive with a holy purpose and with the magnetic power to make others feel the sacredness and beneficence of the cause in which she is engaged, can accomplish in the face of the most disheartening obstacles.

Her school became one of the places in the Capital to be seen, and visitors from all parts of the Union were almost daily to be found there.

Miss Margaret Robinson, of Philadelphia, thus describes her visit : " In the winter of 1853, accompanied by a friend, I visited the school of Myrtilla Miner, under circumstances of peculiar interest.

"Arriving about ten A. M., we learned from a pupil at the door that the teacher was absent on business of importance to the school.

"We were not a little disappointed, supposing all recitations would await her com-

ing. What was our surprise on entering
to find every pupil in her place, closely occupied with her studies. We seated ourselves by polite invitation; soon a class
read; then, one in mental arithmetic exercised itself, the more advanced pupils acting as monitors; all was done without
confusion. When the teacher entered she
expressed no surprise, but took up the business where she found it, and went on. We
learned, subsequently, that this was no unusual thing. On one occasion, being obliged
to leave for several days, she referred to the
scholars the question whether the house
should be closed, or they continue their
exercises without her; they chose the latter. On her return she found all doing
well, not the least disorder having occurred."

In 1855, Miss Miner's health was seriously broken. In writing to a friend of
her condition at that time, she says, under
date of March 4, 1856: "Almost from the
time I last wrote you, I was a pitiable in-

valid, still trying to teach, or, at least, keeping up my school, while really approaching
that stage of nervous sensitiveness and
irritability which ends in insanity. When
reduced to suicidal monomania I yielded to
vacation influences, hoping speedily to re-
cover my usual vigor of body and mind.
But they were too far exhausted, and with
every slight effort I grew worse and worse.
At this stage of affairs, I visited Mrs.
Stowe, who seemed inspired to understand
my state without being told; and, immediately, she employed Horace Mann's sister
to come and take charge of the school one
quarter, and sent me to a water-cure establishment, where I became once more
conscious of life. . . . I am quite well again
except my poor brain, which will not work
well more than three hours a day — nor
three days in a week, when the labor is
continued six hours. This is unlike my
former power, but fortunately, only a few
of my friends know the difference, nor
does my school, so I make my way success-

fully still." And the school, in spite of all
obstacles, did grow and prosper to such an
extent that Miss Miner foresaw, clearly,
that a large building, to be erected on the
permanent site that had been secured,
would soon be absolutely necessary. As
everything depended upon her own personal efforts, she decided to close the school
temporarily, with the twofold object of
recruiting her broken health, and, at the
same time, going about among those interested in the advancement of the colored
race to solicit the means to enlarge the
school. Accordingly in July, 1856, the
school suspended until the autumn of 1857,
when Miss Miner, whose health was not
yet reëstablished, returned, reopened the
school, and transferred the care and teaching of it to a lady (Miss Emily Howland of
Sherwood, New York) whose interest in the
work led her, without any previous experience as a teacher, to volunteer to fill the
unusual and difficult place. Miss Howland
conducted the school until the spring of

1859, when Miss Miner returned to Washington.   Extracts from her letters to Miss Howland, given below, show how she was toiling in the North to get funds with which to erect a suitable building for the school.

In the summer of 1857, she speaks in a letter to Miss Howland of traveling making her "perfectly senseless and sick ; but I have power to recuperate speedily ; therefore I hope and work on."   Again, she says, her "head allows nothing rapid of late."   But all this time she was traveling incessantly, planning or working, talking and writing for her heart's desire.

From Boston, February 9, 1858, she writes to Miss Howland, her associate, "This morning I am to be escorted by Dr. William F. Channing to call upon James Freeman Clarke."

February 10.   "I *did* go yesterday to Jamaica Plain, accompanied by Dr. Channing, to see J. F. Clarke.   The result, aside from my exhaustion to-day, was $100 col-

lected." She speaks, later, of wanting Miss
Howland to send her, from Washington,
"some of those 'dreadful' circulars of
W. H. Beecher's. I have walked myself
so lame, many days I can scarcely move
when night comes, and, sometimes, not
even sit up or talk. But I have collected
$900 in Boston, and a prospect of a thou-
sand more. . . . Saw Dr. Bellows and got
from him a new promise that he will raise
the $1,000, as soon as I get my remaining
$8,000, one of which Dr. Tyng takes, and
I am haunting H. W. Beecher to have him
take another $1,000. I shall try Mr. Chapin
for some hundreds, and hope to have $10,-
000 in hand next October to begin to
build."

In speaking of the "compositions" that
were sent her from the school, she says,
"Now it is not necessary for the colored
people of America to dwell any longer
upon the injustice and inconsistency of
white folks. Their business is to see how
truly noble they can become, regardless of

all wrong — how high they can ascend, and how well they can do. I should like a few essays on general subjects that can be shown to some people who are not flaming Abolitionists. What you have sent will answer for the latter class, and now for the others." But while she was thinking of the greater things she did not forget the lesser, as the following shows. " I think of you with carpets up (it was house - cleaning time at the school) and school - room floors scoured clean, walls whitewashed, and ceilings and windows washed, — in fact, with spring work done. Has Mr. Thomas done the hedge and trimmed the grape-vine, and put the fence in the best possible order ? " Speaking of an intended visitor, she says : " I am anxious you should all appear clean and neat, with bodies washed and heads combed, orderly and quiet in manners ; and the house in perfect order, ornamented with spring flowers." Of her progress, she says : "June 20, 1858. I am getting a new circular printed to send *to everybody.* The Boston people will do well without me all summer. A lady in Worcester has volunteered to collect there, and I am going to Salem and Lynn to find other volunteers." Speaking of a time when her health was temporarily better, she says: "I no longer sigh for death as rest to my uncontrollable weariness, for I have great repose." In another letter she speaks of "that foolish shirking and shrinking from their fate, which destroys the colored youth who promise well. Let them stand firmly and meet all obstacles arising from ignorance and fear among their people." In December, 1858, she writes from Providence, Rhode Island: "It is good, after weeks of severe toil, suffering, meanwhile, from a bad cough, to fall back for a day or two of rest, as I do here, and except my coughing should abate its fury, I shall be kept longer than my wont. . . . I am slowly but surely gathering funds, and *will* have a new *house* next year if it be built with only the $3,000 we have in hand now."

Of Miss Miner's methods in conducting her school a very interesting glimpse may be obtained from the following contribution of a former pupil: —

"I can never cease to be grateful to the memory of Miss Miner for the untold good she has done through her pupils, not only in Washington and vicinity, but wherever they have made their homes. Special thanks are due for the varied training which she gave us. Realizing that there was not sufficient time for each study in its order in our cases, she contrived to give us an insight on many points within a limited space of time.

"As I look back from this period of my life and see how many things I need to know, how much more information I might have had, had I been a more attentive and studious pupil, I am filled with sore regret, because *now* I have no leisure wherein to gain much knowledge.

"Miss Miner gave special attention to the proper writing of letters, and induced a varied correspondence between many prominent persons and her pupils, thus practically bringing her school into larger notice with many of its patrons and friends, and vastly increasing the experience of her pupils. Through her efforts we had correspondence with Dr. Samuel G. Howe, Dr. Orville Dewey, Rev. Charles Ray, and others. Through her we knew many influential and distinguished persons, among whom were Professor and Mrs. Stowe, Hon. Frederick Douglass, Mrs. Julia Ward Howe, Miss Catherine Beecher, and many others.

"At one time Mrs. Horace Mann delivered lectures to the school on some important subject, and her niece, Miss Pennell, gave us drawing lessons. Rev. Moncure D. Conway gave a course of lectures on the "Origin of Words," from which we were required to take copious notes. Mr. Walter W. Johnson also gave us very elaborate lessons in astronomy, and on a few occasions taught us to trace the constellations in the heavens. The last two named subjects possessed a special interest and charm for me.

"Dr. Bailey, of the 'National Era,' was a staunch friend. The family of Secretary Seward and Miss Dodge (Gail Hamilton) were frequent visitors. Hon. Gerrit Smith and his daughter, Mrs. Miller, were also devoted friends.

"Once there was a large fair at the Patent Office, to which the school was taken in a body.

"Dr. and Mrs. Gale, of Washington, were warm friends. On one occasion we visited the doctor's laboratory to witness some interesting philosophical experiments. All these advantages show how untiring were her labors for the welfare and intellectual advancement of her pupils.

"I remember she told my father that she thought slavery would be abolished in less than ten years. He was somewhat incredulous, having always lived in a Southern atmosphere, but they both lived to see emancipation proclaimed by the immortal Lincoln within the prophesied time.

"She obtained for her school, from Northern friends, a large number of newspapers and periodicals at but a nominal cost to ourselves, but which were great helps to increase our knowledge of general matters. She also gathered quite a library, which afforded great benefit and pleasure to her pupils.

"I had the rare pleasure of being intimately associated with her outside of school relations ; have spent many an afternoon and portions of Sabbaths in her company.

"She was a frequent visitor at my father's house, my parents having a high appreciation of her labors in the community. They always made her welcome at their home, and assisted her in many ways.

"I was much impressed with the remembrance of Miss Miner's earnest desire to have erected on the site which she purchased a large building for a 'girls' school,' and how Providence ruled it otherwise.

"The Miner Building is, I believe, especially consecrated to her memory. But the public schools of Washington, in their several handsome buildings, employ among their corps of teachers many of Miss Miner's former pupils, some of whom have been employed since the foundation of the schools. These, in their united and varied work, are building a greater monument to her memory than any one building could.

"Would that I could offer a fitting tribute to her memory. I love and revere her still. This must suffice. 'Her works live after her.' 'Though dead she yet speaketh.'   MATILDA JONES MADDEN."

The school was frequently visited by members of Congress and their families. Among these may be mentioned Schuyler Colfax (afterwards Vice-President of the United States), Joshua R. Giddings, Owen

Lovejoy, and Charles Durkee, of Wisconsin, as taking a special interest. Senator Seward's family were conspicuous in bestowing their friendship and support.

The school was also visited by a number of distinguished clergymen resident in Washington and elsewhere, and received many cordial tributes from them and from others interested in the cause of education.

Senator Henry Wilson, of Massachusetts, afterwards Vice - President of the United States, said, in 1860, in an excited debate in the Senate, in which Jefferson Davis participated, " There is a noble woman here in Washington teaching colored girls." In Mr. Wilson's book, entitled " The Rise and Fall of the Slave Power in America," he says : " The noble woman referred to was Myrtilla Miner, one of the heroines of the irrepressible conflict ; not because she figured largely upon the theatre of popular discussion or entered her public protest against the evils of slavery, but because in the humble walks of the lowly she quietly

7

sought out, and with patient and protracted
effort educated, the children of the pro-
scribed and prostrate race." Mr. Wilson
then sketches briefly the incidents of Miss
Miner's life as given in this memoir, and
closes with the following eloquent tribute:
" There is something touchingly impressive in the life and purpose of Miss Miner.
In the great and grim tragedy of human
affairs they afforded a delightful episode.
In this selfish world — with its grasping and
jostling throng — she seemed like some
angel ministrant on her mission of mercy.
On the dark background of the nation's
history it seemed an illuminated picture
resplendent with truthfulness and love.
Her life of romantic incident was at once
redolent and beautiful. It was in itself a
sweet poem, a living evangel of a heart
yearning towards humanity, and filled with
a sublime trust in God." [1]

Some time in 1860 the school appears

---

[1] *Rise and Fall of the Slave Power in America.* Vol. ii. pp.
583–586.

to have closed. The shadows of the approaching conflict were deepening on the horizon; the blasts of opposition were so fierce, the elements on every hand were so threatening, that, in her shattered health, she felt incapable of breasting the storm which she had long known must come sooner or later. In 1856, writing to a dear friend, she had predicted it in these words: " I begin to have previsions that Fremont will not be elected — then, forebodings of civil war and your danger in Washington. I believe it is coming as I believe my life."

In 1861 she went to California, mainly with a view to the restoration of her health. While there she met with a serious accident, and returned to die in Washington, in 1864, as will be related in the next chapter.

While Miss Miner was absent in California her friends in Washington were not idle; and Congress, relieved at last of its pro-slavery incubus by the secession of the South, easily passed, in 1863 (Mr. Wilson

introducing it in the Senate, February 17,
1863), an act for the incorporation of the
Institution for the Education of Colored
Youth in the District of Columbia, thus
putting, at last, the national seal and sanc-
tion on the labors of so many years of
prayer and struggle. We give the act of
incorporation below : —

[Chapter 103.   Act of March 3, 1863, U. S. Stats. at L.,
v. 12, p. 796.]

*An Act to incorporate the Institution for the Edu-
cation of Colored Youth in the District of
Columbia.*

Be it enacted by the Senate and House
of Representatives of the United States
of America in Congress assembled, that
Henry Addison, John C. Underwood,
George C. Abbott,[1] William H. Channing,
Nancy M. Johnson, of the District of
Columbia, and Myrtilla Miner, of Califor-
nia, and their associates and successors,

---

[1] The name of Mr. Abbott is incorrectly given in the act as passed.
It should have been George J. Abbot.

are hereby constituted and declared to be
a body politic and corporate, by the name
and title of " The Institution for the Education of Colored Youth," to be located in
the District of Columbia ; the objects of
which institution are to educate and improve the moral and intellectual condition
of such of the colored youth of the nation as
may be placed under its care and influence,
and by that name shall have perpetual suc-
cession, with power to sue and be sued, to
plead and be impleaded, in any court of
the United States, to collect subscriptions,
make by-laws, rules, and regulations, as
may be needful for the government of said
institution, and the same to alter, amend,
and abrogate at pleasure ; to have a com-
mon seal, the same to break, alter, and re-
new at will ; to appoint such officers as
may be required for the management of
the institution, and to assign them their
duties, and generally to provide for the
transaction of all business appertaining to
said institution. And the by - laws and

regulations which may be so adopted shall be as valid as if they were made a part of this act : *Provided,* They shall not be inconsistent herewith, nor repugnant to the laws of the District of Columbia.

SECTION 2. *And be it further enacted,* That said corporation may have, hold, and receive, for the purpose of said institution, and for no other, real, personal, and mixed estate, by purchase, gift, or devise, not to exceed one hundred thousand dollars ; to use, lease, sell, or convey the same for the purposes and benefit of said institution ; may appoint such teachers as may be necessary, and fix their compensation.

SECTION 3. *And be it further enacted,* That said corporation shall not be engaged in any banking or commercial business, nor shall it issue any note, check, or other evidence of debt intended to be used as a circulation ; and Congress may have the right to alter or repeal this act at any time hereafter.

Approved March 3, 1863.

The corporators organized soon after the act was passed, and chose additional members, but it was not until February, 1871, that arrangements were completed by which the school was continued. This was first accomplished in connection with Howard University, of Washington, D. C., where a Preparatory and Normal Department was organized under the control of that institution, but supported from the funds collected by Miss Miner.

In May, 1872, the square of ground (No. 115) which was purchased in 1853 for four thousand dollars was sold by the corporators of the "Institution for the Education of Colored Youth" for forty thousand dollars. This sum, with the other funds that had accumulated, gave an assured annual income of about three thousand dollars, and it was felt by the corporators that greater usefulness would be attained if the school should assume a more independent existence. So the arrangement with Howard University was terminated, and on the

13th of September, 1876, the Miner Normal School was reopened in a leased building, No. 1613 P St., N. W.

Soon the need of more extensive and independent accommodations was so imperiously felt that the corporators decided to erect a school building of their own, which was accomplished in 1877 at a cost of thirty-seven thousand dollars. This fine and commodious building, situated on 17th Street, between P and Q streets, with the lot on which it stands, was wholly paid for out of the Miner Fund, and is called the Miner School Building. By an arrangement with the School Trustees of the District of Columbia, that portion of the building not occupied by the Normal School was leased at an annual rental to the District of Columbia for other colored schools.

The dedication of the new building took place October 18, 1877, with appropriate and interesting ceremonies. Rev. William Henry Channing, Miss Miner's friend and counselor for many years, and whose office it was to say, as only he could say, the fitting words at her burial, was happily able to be present and make the dedicatory address. He drew an inspiring picture of the future of the colored race on this continent, was eloquent throughout, and, at times, deeply touching. Frederick Douglass, the most eloquent and distinguished member of the colored race present, and one of the most powerful of American orators, white or black, made a glowing and impassioned speech, in which he embodied the account of Miss Miner's visit to him while seeking for aid, which is given in his letter in the early part of this memoir.

The school was reopened on P Street under the care of Miss Mary B. Smith, of Beverly, Massachusetts, as principal. Miss Smith and her sister, Miss Sarah R. Smith, continued the school when later it was removed to the new building, until they were succeeded by Miss M. B. Briggs, in September, 1879. Miss Briggs was succeeded by Miss Lucy E. Moten, in September, 1883.

The first treasurer of the institution after it organized under the act of incorporation was Francis George Shaw, of Staten Island, New York. He was succeeded by George E. Baker, formerly of Washington, now of New York, who still continues in that office, and to whom the institution is under many obligations for his careful and able management of its finances.

The present Board of Corporators is composed as follows: Mrs. Nancy M. Johnson, President; George E. Baker, Treasurer; Mrs. Ellen M. O'Connor, Secretary; Walker Lewis, Caroline B. Winslow, M. D., Frederick Douglass, Miss Emily J. Brigham, Mrs. Mary J. Stroud, and Rev. Rush R. Shippen.

By an arrangement with the Trustees of the Public Schools of the District of Columbia, consummated in 1879, it was agreed that the Miner Normal School should bear the same relation to the Board of Trustees of Public Schools and pupils of the colored schools of the District of Columbia as then existed between the Washington Normal School (for whites) and pupils of the white schools of said District.

Since the above arrangement was consummated, by which the school became a part of the colored school system of the District of Columbia, and up to June, 1884, eighty-two young women have graduated from it,[1] sixty-four of whom are now employed as teachers in the public schools of the District of Columbia; eight have retired after service in the schools; two have died while in the service, and several are now teaching elsewhere. It is acknowledged that the colored schools of the District have been much benefited by being furnished in this manner with trained professional teachers.

Miss Miner, referring to the high standard she had always held up for the guidance

[1] On the 4th of June, 1885, sixteen more young women graduated from the Miner Normal School.

of the school, says in one of her letters:
" But it becomes me to candidly confess
my continuous weakness (if weakness it
be) in not having reduced my standard of
excellence for that school; and I would
rather see it suspended forever than continued on reduced principles, indulging the
weaknesses and deteriorating elements of
character which attend all oppressed
classes." It is a pleasure to be able to
state that under successive able principals
the standard of excellence upheld by Miss
Miner has not been allowed to deteriorate,
and that the school will compare favorably
with white schools of the same grade in any
part of the Union. And the institution
bids fair to continue for many years in the
future to exalt and perpetuate the memory
of its founder, and be a continual blessing
to the community where it exists.

VI.

Personal Traits. — Close of a Noble Life.

HER personal appearance is thus described by one who knew her intimately. "Miss Miner was a fascinating woman. She had bright brown eyes, a pale, clear skin, an aquiline nose, and a graceful neck. Her beautiful dark brown hair she always wore in curls, forming a frame on each side of her pale but animated face. She was well built, of about medium height, chest rather broad, with shoulders which gave her a vigorous look despite her habitual ill health. To this she never gave way. She was full of personal magnetism, and never failed to impress deeply all with whom she came in contact."

Says the friend who afterwards became her valued assistant in the school work : —

" She was often severe in her kindness,
as, no doubt, many of her old pupils will
remember. Perfectly intolerant of bad
odors, because the result of generations of
unwashed bodies ; perfectly indifferent to
the luxurious meals often prepared for her
in the homes of her pupils, because of the
untidiness of those homes ; it must be said
of her, as of many a spirited teacher before
her, that she was not always patient of
spirit. She grudged waiting for results ;
she wanted her scholars to attain at once
to be very beautiful in body and mind. In
her tremendous efforts to compass this object she exhausted her physical strength.
She used up, and often wasted, her vitality
for those whom she would see lifted up a
little, even if she died in the attempt to
raise them. I remember two little girls
who came with her from Washington, and
who traveled with her extensively through
the North. How scrupulously neat she
obliged them to be, and how sensitive she
was on their account, as much so, it seemed

to me, as if they had been her own children. She could not, without great grief to herself, have any one remember that they belonged to a despised race. They were everything to her, and she watched them with jealous care.

"She was impatient of the prejudice which was found with some, and could hardly wait for it to subside. If those little girls lived to womanhood, and are still living, they must often remember her tender care for them and her affectionate solicitude."

Opening one of Miss Miner's letters to this lady, who was in charge of her school during one of her absences, one can hardly help a smile at finding a wood-cut of what school-girls would call some "horrid things," and written upon it by Miss Miner, "Animalculæ of the teeth, for the girls to examine who neglect to clean theirs daily;" evidently torn from an advertising circular of some wonderful tooth powder.

Miss Miner's extraordinary strictness in

the matter of personal cleanliness may be further illustrated by the following characteristic extract from a letter written by her to a young colored woman, who, as will be seen, contemplated coming to Washington to assist her in the school: "You seem willing to come, but I hope you consider how exceedingly particular I am; that I require every scholar to bathe all over every day, and should not like a person in my house who would neglect it; indeed, I would not live with one who was careless in her personal habits."

"Miss Miner was a spirited teacher," says the friend quoted before. "Her whole living was intense, and there was but little repose about her. I have a distinct recollection that whenever she was with me she kept me alive all over. But whatever else she was, she was unquestionably the true friend of the then despised colored race; and whatever else she did or did not do, she labored for that race, and groaned in spirit for them."

Her ideals of life were exalted and pure, and the intensity of moral purpose which enabled her to accomplish such a noble work in the world finds energetic expression in the following extract from one of her letters: "*Character* is what the age calls for; character that dare do a noble deed; that can outlive the ebb tide of a false world's judgment; that can be true to God and man and leave the result. Oh, 'the opinion of the world,' I hate it! I would despise myself more than I do now were I bound by it. It is not true to manhood, or to womanhood, or to humanity. If you can do a good deed or a noble or a true one, *do it.* Care not for the 'opinion of the world.' Keep your own heart pure and true; that will secure to you a higher, holier opinion than all the world combined could bestow. You and God are the beings involved as having any opinion of consequence. What should you care for any other? Self-consciousness of good or evil is the great law, and the only

8

one for which you or I shall be held responsible before the Judge of the quick and the dead."

Writing to a young man who had gone to Lake Superior to live and work, under date of February 11, 1855, she says: "That glorious aurora, it is worth living in Lake Superior a year to behold! and my enthusiasm would almost make me also willing to watch all night in ecstatic delight. I am so glad you love nature; it is an everlasting resource. Love it still, I pray you; love simplicity in childlike confidence, and truth in holy faith. . . . I would have yours a great, true, noble manhood! God has made you of very nice material, and if you will let Him, He will refine you without the fire of affliction. He will make you pure, and holy, and good enough to live on earth, and bless and be blessed. You have but to cherish the good that is in you, and let it overpower the evil, so that your mind may see all light and all truth, and you will immediately become one of nature's nobility, and no man can question the origin of your aristocracy, for it is above his ken, except he belong to the same household, and receive his inheritance from the Almighty. . . .

"Above all, whatever else may betide, pray the good Lord to save you from ever sinking so low as to become a Northern doughface [1] — the meanest thing that God permits to live! . . . As I have no doubt you are to become an important item in the 'State of Superior,' I hope you may cultivate enough of your religious element to pray in faith, shown by works, an anti-doughface prayer that will be heard and answered all your life long."

A lady who was a pupil of Miss Miner's when she taught in Smethport Academy, in 1850 says: "As the time passed on, we saw embodied in our teacher a character entirely original and independent in its relations to human judgments and worldly

---

[1] A Northern man with Southern principles; an apologist for slavery.

considerations, but grandly responsive to any demands that were made by human needs, and to all commands that were recognized as coming from the Father of All." . . .

"The pupils of this true teacher were enriched by highest principles of character building, and they were aided in grasping the grand ideas of the dignity of human nature and of the brotherhood of all in human form. Was it not just like this large-hearted woman to visit the prisoners in our county jail and sing to them, thinking that kindly words, accompanied by the sweetness of music, might, in some way, suggest to them One who had power and willingness to loosen fetters of sin, and thus make free indeed?"

It is not surprising to learn that one who so passionately believed in education and freedom for the colored race insisted with the same earnestness upon equal rights for woman, in all social and political relations.

A friend says that Miss Miner was in

the habit, every Fourth of July, of writing a protest against the celebration of the day, for she declared that it had not proclaimed the equality and independence of woman. On one occasion she wrote an eloquent letter on this theme to the friend quoted, — Dr. Caroline B. Winslow, — and in it expressed the idea that the liberation of the negro must come first, and then the enfranchisement of woman. It is deeply regretted that this letter has been lost, thus making it impossible to give her language in full.

One who was intimate with her the latter part of her life writes : " It was in the year 1855 that my acquaintance with Miss Miner began. We met at the house of a friend where I was spending some days, — a part of my summer vacation. It was in July or August. She also was sojourning in the same city, Providence, Rhode Island, and came to my friend's home a few days before I left. I was at once struck with her appearance, and intensely interested in

her as a woman, and in her plans and purposes, of which I had heard through our
mutual friend, Mrs. Paulina Wright Davis,
our hostess.

" I wish that I were capable of painting
her portrait so as to make another see her
as she looked then and afterward.   To say
that her eyes were lustrous and brown
gives no idea of the depth and variety of
expression in them.   They were at times
the most gentle and smiling of eyes ; again,
upon occasions when her indignation was
aroused, they were capable of expressing
terrible wrath, as some of the ruffians and
rowdies who insulted her girls could testify.

" Her hair was brown and glossy, her skin
clear, and all her features good.   She was,
I think, of rather less than medium height,
and thin, but not what one would call a
slight frame ; and she gave the impression
from the first of great power, — mental,
moral, and spiritual ; but seemed at that
time to be utterly worn and exhausted ;
so much so in fact, that she had been for-

bidden by her physician to talk about her work; yet she could not avoid the subject, for every one with whom she came in contact wanted to hear of just that; and she found it quite impossible to get the desired rest for her weary brain.

"She was hoping to gather up her strength to start again, with new vigor, to collect money and erect the buildings. This kind of work required much talking, and answering of questions, and great expenditure of vitality, in going from place to place, and from person to person.

"Her face and figure expressed, more than any other that the writer ever saw, that which she herself admired, — 'character,' power, individuality. There was a sense of her being thoroughly alive; not restless, but fully and keenly alive. It distinguished her even at this time when she was so worn with her labors that she was prostrated in health.

"I very soon observed Miss Miner's great love of flowers and children, and her uncommon ability to charm and interest children, her exquisite tact — which is another name for sympathy — in dealing with them. All children seemed instinctively to love her.

" It was a part of her daily, self-appointed task, while at the home of our friend, to gather and arrange the flowers in the vases, for our hostess had a lovely garden and flower-beds. Every morning while engaged in this occupation I watched and followed her closely to catch any word that she might drop, so fascinated was I by her exquisite and delicate personality and ways, united with such a strong character as hers seemed to me. Indeed, I now suspect that I must have almost shadowed her footsteps. I remember, however, that she seemed to enjoy my companionship and my interest in her work.

" Some weeks later she came to my home in Boston, much refreshed from her stay in Providence, and together we went to see persons from whom she hoped to

get contributions for the school. Her
health was not, however, for some time
sufficiently established to resume her labors in the school, and a part of the
autumn of 1855 and of the winter of 1856
were spent at the Elmira Water Cure with
her dear and valued friends Doctors S. O.
and R. B. Gleason, who took the deepest interest in her, and were ever after among
her most helpful and sympathizing friends."

In October, 1861, she went to California,
mainly for her health, but hoping and in-
tending to collect funds for the school.
She supported herself while there as a
clairvoyant and magnetic healer, for which
vocations she seems to have had a considerable gift, recently developed. At first
she resided in San Francisco, and afterwards she made extensive journeys over
the State, and enjoyed its splendid scenery,
which to her was a constant delight. Writing to the friend last quoted, from Taylors-
ville, Plumas County, California, under date
of December 16, 1863, she says : " I have

left my very pleasant, sunny rooms at San
Francisco for the mountains again, and
am nestled in a lovely valley surrounded
by hills, which hills, with their ravines,
stretch off into vast mountains overtopped
by everlasting snows.   I am doubtless two
hundred or three hundred miles northeast
from San Francisco, with mountains inter-
vening which will not let me out before
next June, except by saddle or dog train.
. . . One thing is certain, that I am carried
about this country to see and enjoy its
magnificent scenery in a most remarkable
manner, without any care or expense, save
my time and talents, which pay for all.   In
coming here to this valley we came from
San Francisco to Sacramento by steam-
boat, thence to Marysville by stage (the
water being too low to risk the boat lest
we get aground and suffer delay), then a
long day's ride over eighty miles of rough
road, in a Concord wagon, — from four A. M.
to ten P. M., — then up next morning at five
to ride ten miles on mule-back to break-

fast, then twenty miles more the same day over the most fearful heights of the Sierra Nevadas. I had no idea of coming the way we did, and had I had the slightest conception of the danger should not have consented. But I had the joy of finding my little mule sure-footed over the snowy, rocky trail, so frightful that not a man of all the seven in our company dared ride down it; but I kept my seat, and got safe through. Some of the way the snow was four feet deep over the trail, and each mule set his feet exactly in the steps of his predecessor; yet down some of the steeps it was very slippery, and my poor mule slipped his hind feet entirely under him, and slid thus some yards, but finally raised himself, very easy, without dismounting me. This was while we were passing at the foot of Pilot Peak, one of the highest peaks of all the Sierras. Then we were on rocky, narrow, stair-like steeps, where the least false step of the mule would have thrown us into interminable depths. We

passed over three of these immense heights,
one of which took us down a continuous,
very steep, zigzag trail of four miles, down,
down, fearfully down, to the river, over
rocks and rough foot-bridges, — no wagon
road, — and then again up, up the moun-
tain sides beyond, till I was all chafed and
mauled and pummeled, so that I could not
move without groaning for pain for many
days and nights, but was *glad* all the time."

Her experiences in California were destined to have a tragic ending. An accident which finally resulted in her death
is described by her in a letter to the same
friend, dated Petaluma, California, May 5,
1864. After referring to some business
details relating to the affairs of the school,
the letter is interrupted and begins again
thus: "It is now the first of June. Two
days after the above was written I received
a delightful letter from Dr. Bellows which
I designed answering in person very soon.
The following morning my friend planned
an all day's ride for us. A friend of

hers escorted me in one carriage, and
she accompanied her son in another. My
escort came with a fine span of black
ponies and light buggy to match, and I
entered it with much exhilaration of feeling, for I greatly enjoy fast driving. The
horses started upon the jump, ran, leaped!
flew!! the road turning two short corners
and leading by their stable, and within
twenty rods of this house we were thrown
thirty feet in the air, falling with a crash,
I alighting on my right hip with greatest
force, and so spraining it that very little
motion of any kind has since characterized
me. I was otherwise bruised, but not muti-
lated, fractured, or broken, save my clothes;
yet all sinks to insignificance compared
with this loss of locomotion. I was compelled to keep my bed until I became very
nervous from inaction, suffering from con-
gestion of the whole right side and fever,
until it culminated last week in a profuse
hemorrhage of the right lung, which reduced me very low. I am rallying again,

— slowly moving about, leaning upon a cane, and longing to get home once more; but this calamity has nearly obliterated all my great health and vigor which I had gathered as a full harvest in the mountains, feeling sure the supply would meet the demand of any labor which might await me on my return. I was full of courage and ready for anything, as agile and strong as ever in my life. This has greatly changed me. My aspect is that of a hopeless consumptive, and my feelings subdued and careless. I am now very, very weak, yet I hope much from the sea voyage. It will kill or cure me; I feel quite indifferent which. Starr King has gone — Owen Lovejoy has gone — and to-day, I see Joshua R. Giddings has gone. We have all worked well, and I shall find company with whom I can still work to great advantage 'on the other side of Jordan.'"

After a journey which was made by steamer in those days, including transshipment across the Isthmus of Panama,

and which must have taxed severely the
endurance and strength of a person in her
feeble and suffering condition, she arrived
in New York in August, 1864. After
tarrying some time with friends in the
East, with no permanent improvement in
health, she came to Washington in December, 1864, to the house of Mrs. Nancy M.
Johnson, now President of the Board of
Trustees of the Miner School, where in
ten days she died. During these last ten
days of her life it was the privilege of the
writer to spend a portion of some of them
with her, answering her letters and listen-
ing to her plans, — when her cough would
permit her to talk, — for she at times felt
that she might yet be well and work again.
Her faith in her recovery was strong almost to the last. She enjoyed communion
with invisible friends, and was very happy
in such communion. But the end was
near, and on the 17th of December, 1864,
at the age of forty-nine, Myrtilla Miner
passed onward to her reward. Who can

doubt that on that other shore she heard
the welcoming voice of the Master, saying,
Well done, good and faithful daughter!
Enter thou into the joy of thy Lord!

Rev. William Henry Channing, then pastor of the Unitarian Church of Washington,
and an old and valued friend, conducted
the funeral services. After the services
her remains were taken to the beautiful
Oak Hill cemetery in Georgetown, and
placed in the receiving vault. Falling
snow whitened the ground and dropped in
light, feathery flakes upon the open grave
as her body was laid away, two weeks later,
in its final resting-place. Miss Howland
tells a very touching incident connected
with Miss Miner's burial. Mrs. Johnson,
her friend, after the coffin was lowered,
bent forward over the grave and expressed
the greatest desire to look once more upon
the dead face. One of the attendants immediately got down into the grave and removed the coffin-lid, so that the face was
in full sight. She looked so natural and

so beautiful, it seemed as if she were only sleeping. The long, brown curls from one side had fallen partly over one cheek and lay across the throat. A strange and lovely sight, never to be forgotten by those who witnessed it.

Miss Miner's grave at Oak Hill has not yet been marked by a memorial stone. The recent formation of an Alumni Society, composed of the graduates of the Miner School, suggests the thought that the members of such an association might fitly take the matter in hand, and, with a small contribution from each, do lasting honor to themselves by erecting an appropriate monument to the memory of their bene-factress.

9

THE SCHOOL

FOR

COLORED GIRLS.

WASHINGTON, D. C.

PHILADELPHIA:

MERRIHEW & THOMPSON'S STEAM POWER PRESS,

Merchant Street above Fourth.

1854.

TO THE READERS OF THE FOLLOWING ADDRESS.

The undersigned have purchased, in the City of Washington, a large lot, with two small houses, which they hold in trust for the use and benefit of the COLORED GIRLS' SCHOOL, now under the charge of Myrtilla Miner. Including various expenses and some interest on money borrowed, the cost of the property is $4,300. The Trustees have received funds to the amount of $2,500; of which one thousand dollars were contributed by Harriet B. Stowe, $250 by Jasper Cope of Philadelphia, $150 by the Trustees of the Murray Fund, New York, and the balance by many other persons, in various sums. To discharge the debt incurred for the property and erect a suitable building for the accommodation of the School, it is estimated that it will be necessary to raise the further sum of about $8,000.

Contributions to this fund are respectfully solicited and will be gladly received by M. MINER, in Washington, and by

THOMAS WILLIAMSON,
S. W. Corner of Arch and Seventh streets.
SAMUEL RHOADS,
No. 50 North Fourth Street, Philadelphia.

First month 20th, 1854.

ADDRESS.

DEAR FRIENDS,—

We come to you with no array of logic, but with words of simple truth. Will you hear us, and then "prove all things, and hold fast that which is good?"

The Second Anniversary of the "Colored Girls' School," opened in the city of Washington, D. C., December 3d, 1851, has arrived, and it is thought best, by those interested for its success, to present to your consideration some facts connected with its establishment. Two years have been allowed to pass, that we might ourselves become fully satisfied with the feasibility of the plan and the probability of its permanency and usefulness, and we are now prepared to speak with a confidence that must be acceptable to all who sincerely pray—"Thy kingdom come, thy will be done on earth as it is done in heaven."

The first promptings to *this* effort, to educate the free colored population of the country, were suggested by a Southern *Christian*, who unequivocally asserted that this was the truest and safest method of relieving the country of those vexed questions which disturb its peace and agitate its leading minds.

In this city alone, may be found a population of more than 8000 free colored people, not prohibited by any law from obtaining a complete education, and there may be nearly 2000 children of suitable age to attend school.

Two years ago the Colored Girls' School opened with six children; the number increased to fifteen during the first month, and during the second to forty, which has been the average number since; the school having been limited to this number from the impossibility of securing larger rooms.

There were previously five or six private schools in the District taught by colored men, from which some of these girls professed to have graduated, *i. e.* learned all their instructors could teach them. But they were unable to apply the knowledge they had acquired to any practical use. While professing to be able to read well, they had no proper understanding of what they read ; while professing to understand grammar, they rarely spoke or wrote good English; while professing to have advanced through practical arithmetic, they could neither read nor write numbers accurately, nor keep accounts with any correctness. These graduates were from fifteen to seventeen years of age, and unfortunately, some of them very uncultivated in mind and manners; and their pride was so shocked when they were thrown into classes with *children* who were acquiring first principles, that every one, the good as well as the bad, *left school* after six months or a year, and all returned to their various avocations, quite unwilling to assume the responsibility of teaching, though they had entered the school with the full understanding, that it was established to educate a class of girls particularly for that profession.

Fortunately, a younger and more morally healthful class remained, and were soon joined by others of similar ages, habits and impressible minds. These, with few changes, now compose the very interesting school each day assembled, pursuing the various studies calculated to enlighten their minds, refine their tastes, cultivate proper habits, and develop all their powers for usefulness and happiness. These earnest seekers after knowledge, have thus far advanced nobly, and some of them, by the manifestation of superior talents, more than answer the expectations of their teachers. They cheerfully respond to every effort made on their behalf, and seem to appreciate the privileges afforded them for acquiring such an education as shall render them independent in the duties that devolve on them in future life. We can give no pledges for the future, but the *present promise* is, that when these girls are mature, many of them will become teachers, and by their refinement and good morals exert such an influence upon their associates, as shall relieve the world of much degradation and consequent misery.

Having been a teacher of white children for twenty years, I may be allowed an opinion respecting the capacity of these colored children, and I do unequivocally assert, that I find no difference of native talent, where similar advantages are enjoyed, between Anglo-Saxons and Africo-Americans. Indeed, if we accept the historical testimony of Hon. Edward Everett, in his address before the American Colonization Society, delivered at Washington, D. C., Jan.

18th, 1853, we must conclude, that the ancestors of Europeans were at one time not very unlike the Africans, for he says: "It is only ten centuries since the Anglo-Saxons, to whose race we are so fond of claiming kindred, were as barbarous and uncivilized as many of the African tribes." Then may we not with much propriety inquire, why should their descendents in America be found so very dissimilar? Again, admitting Dr. Orville Dewey's still broader basis of reasoning, which proves that the colored races possess all *human attributes*, and are therefore entitled to all lawful and proper means of development, if not in as high degree, yet fundamentally the same as ourselves,—God having so constituted us that it becomes *a duty* to seek the highest good of our better nature,—we may most emphatically ask why the colored people of America, and particularly those of Washington, D. C., (one half of whom are three-fourths white,) may not have schools, *free schools*, the same as any other class of citizens? and why, since the *city* refuses to recognize them as a part of the public, and grants them no privileges, except those of being *taxed* without a representation, and *punished* for violating laws which they have no voice in enacting, why should not the *nation's legislators* nobly bestow upon this faithful class of laborers, the means of an appropriate education? *Faithful* they unquestionably are, and comprising, as they do, nearly one fourth the resident population of this District, why should such a suffering mass appear unworthy the notice of Congress? Miss Dix nobly pleads for the criminal and insane—but we plead for the *workers*, upon whom the personal comfort of all so much depends, that *they may be saved from crime or insanity* by the removal of those fearful maladies—ignorance and want. Our country has funds enough to bestow for the relief of all her poor, and may she first be *just*, then generous !

While good men send forth ship-loads of bread to feed the famishing of other lands, and the country sends full equipments of ships, money and men to bear home the oppressed of other nations; why not remember the sufferers at home whom the Pharaohs of injustice require "to make bricks without straw ?" These suffer for want of soul-food ! for enlightenment of mind ! such as a Christian nation should be careful to bestow, ere it require strict obedience to its laws !

Friends, these hard-handed workers will in time become physically strong—and, if left in *ignorance*, no wise counsel can stay the tide, should they rise in their might and desperation, to roll back the flood of power that deprives them of privileges, which, ignorant as they are, they know to be the "inalienable right" of every honest person who treads American soil. This *you* have taught them without schools, and now they must be enlightened, and awakened to a full consciousness of things as they are; of the difficulties to be met, and of the best mode of disposing of them.

They should be imbued with a high order of Christianity, (which may God grant,) and with principles of love and peace; for, after much reflection, we are sure that nothing less than proper instruction, accompanied by *justice to these people*, can ward off the evils shrouded in the future, and which surely await *us*, if we refuse to listen to the voice of reason and the direction of the Divine Teacher, "as ye would that men should do to you, do ye even so to them."

Shall the colored people of Washington be allowed the instruction necessary to enlighten their minds, awaken their consciences and purify their lives?

We fear some will answer "no," but there are others who will say "*yes*," and to these we earnestly look for aid.

Friends, you are no longer without a precedent. The Colored Girls' School has enjoyed uninterrupted continuance and *success* during two years, with no earthly dependence save the will of a single individual, an entire stranger in the community to both white and colored, with only such aids as could be obtained from a few individuals; and no accommodations except the small inconvenient rooms which very limited means would afford.

But God, the Father of us all, kindly watched over those whom He had sent, so that both scholars and teachers have been preserved in safety, and "not a sparrow permitted to fall to the ground without His notice."

The majesty of righteousness has surrounded the school, and a power unseen has guarded all its ways, so that many "scorners have passed by on the other side," and the universal testimony, where truth prevails over penurious strife, has been that "*this is right.*"

What has been accomplished by human agency, has involved some personal sacrifice, much stern toil and deprivation, and all the *aid* kind friends have been willing to bestow. But means to perfect the establishment are still requisite, for there is a multitude to be taught, and few comparatively can read or secure the means to pay for learning. It is literally a missionary field, as truly as any where light and truth are required to instruct and relieve suffering humanity.

Parents often come, saying, " will you take my daughter into your school? *I* cannot read even the Bible, but I want her taught, so that she can read it to me."

It has often been necessary to reply " there is no more room. I cannot find space for another scholar at present, and you must wait awhile." " But," they urge, " my daughter is just now the age to be in school, and soon she must be at work to earn her living, and help her parents educate the other children." One father came, bringing a fine looking child, about nine years old, fairer than many who claim pure Anglo-Saxon origin, and presented her to me, saying, " will you educate my daughter? I have so many children I can hardly feed and clothe them, much less give them learning, but I want this one taught ; and if you will educate her you may have her." The answer was, " yes, I will teach her, if you will not prevent her being a teacher or a missionary." There are constantly in attendance a number of such promising beneficiaries, sometimes amounting to ten. This takes all the charity-pence from the teachers' pockets, for they are entirely dependent on a low tuition for support. It is fixed at $15 per annum : books, etc. being furnished gratuitously, which, in a city of vast expenses like this, where " each one seeks his own, and not the things of another," is too low a price to afford even necessary comforts to the school, much less to the teachers who strictly guard against any discomfort to the pupils.

Publishers and other friends have done good service, by their contributions of papers, periodicals and books. A library of about 500 volumes has been collected, contributed principally by publishers in New York and Boston, and *Friends* in Philadelphia, which with the 12 weekly and semi-weekly papers, 26 monthlies and semi-monthlies now sent to the school, afford means of acquiring general information, never previously granted to the colored people of

Washington. All these aid the teachers much in awakening intelligent thoughts in the minds of the pupils, as have also the lectures on History, Drawing, Analysis, Philosophy and Astronomy, delivered by kind friends in Washington, for all of which we return many, *many thanks*, expressive of our full appreciation of these favors, and also our desire for their continuance.

Partial sets of class books have repeatedly been given to the school, but the classes have so far exceeded the number contributed that it has been necessary to expend from $5 to $25 at different times to complete the sets.

From the fact that the school was visited during the first four months of 1853, by more than one hundred persons, from various parts of the country, and by some many times, we hope a healthful influence may be widely disseminated and prove beneficial to other localities beside Washington.

The rent of rooms is at present $9 per month, fuel from $10 to $12 per month during the winter, board $12, assistant teacher the meagre sum of $16 ; the expenses being sometimes more than the income, so that often nothing is left to replenish the ever-wasting wardrobes. Could each one of the forty pupils pay promptly $1.50 per month, the current expenses might be met, but some promising ones cannot pay at all; some can pay only a part, and some necessarily put far away the paying day, so that there would often be great scarcity did not "the Lord provide" by the careful hand of his children, whom He teacheth to "remember the poor when they cry, the fatherless and him that hath none to help him." We would at this time considerately inquire, can we be sustained in our efforts to perfect an Institution of learning here, adequate to the wants of the people, worthy the enlightened spirit of the age, and embodying those religious principles and moral teachings, which, by their fruits, shall be found to purify the heart, rendering it "first pure, then peaceable?"

We have endeavored to lay before you the school with all its interests; the efforts already made on its behalf; the successful results; the difficulties yet to be met, and the hopes of the future ; and since it appears that in this incipient stage, the school can scarcely sustain its own internal workings, and that we must depend upon the friends of the cause to secure for us a permanent place, and erect suitable buildings adapted to the wants of the school, our appeal is designed for this purpose—earnestly praying " our Father in heaven " to enlarge the hearts of his children to a prompt and full answering.

Faithfully submitted on behalf of the School.

M. MINER, Teacher.

TESTIMONIALS.

☞ In sending forth this appeal, it seems proper that it should be accompanied with a few of the many testimonials which have been kindly furnished by friends who have visited the School, and the following are therefore appended, with one on behalf of the Teacher :—

WHITESVILLE, Wilkinson Co., Miss., May 31, 1848.

Know all whom it may concern, that Miss Myrtilla Miner has for more than twelve months been assistant in the Newton Institute which is under my charge—that most of the time she had the whole care of the School—that she has manifested as a Teacher and a Governess the highest moral character and unusual skill in imparting knowledge, arousing thought and disciplining in the most rational manner, while her character at all times has been most unexceptionable.   D. L. PHARES, A. M.
Principal of Newton Institute.

From the Hon. Charles Durkee, late Member of Congress, Wisconsin.

" I am familiar with the history of a superior Colored School lately established in the city of Washington, by the persevering and untiring energy of Miss Miner, and I have been highly pleased with the rapid advances her scholars have made in the various branches of study assigned them, and take great pleasure in commending this highly benevolent and philanthropic undertaking to the favorable consideration of the good and liberal everywhere."

WASHINGTON, July, 1852.

From the Hon. Norton S. Townshend, late Member of Congress, Ohio.

" Having visited Miss Miner's School for Colored Girls in Washington, D. C., I take great pleasure in bearing testimony to its character and success. I believe I have never visited a school where greater anxiety to learn was manifested by the pupils, or greater progress demonstrated ; nor do I know of a teacher better fitted for her task, or an enterprise more worthy of encouragement."

WASHINGTON, July, 1852.

From the Hon. Mrs. J. Horsford, Livingston Co. N. Y.

" I have been a frequent visitor at Miss Miner's School for Colored Girls since December last. It has been an object of much interest to me since the commencement, and the uniform good order of the School and the application of the pupils have been very gratifying. I have been particularly interested with their clear narration of the contents of the books which they receive from the library : I have never heard better. I have been also pleased with their reading, and, in this respect, think they excel any district School I have ever seen. They are very ready in mental arithmetic and excel in other branches. I cannot but view this School as destined to exert a great influence for good in the future. Whether as teachers here or as principals of female seminaries in Liberia, the instruction they now receive will enable them to fill either station with respectability, and with great good to those who may come under their influence."

WASHINGTON, June 23d, 1852.

From the Rev. S. P. Hill, Pastor of the 10th St. Baptist Church, Washington.

" I have visited Miss Miner's School, and fully agree with all that is attested of its excellence in the foregoing testimonials."

WASHINGTON, July, 1852.

From the Rev. J. B. Grinnell, formerly Pastor of the First Congregational Church, Washington, D. C., now of the Congregational Church, 4th St., New York.

" I visited Miss Miner's School several times during the first month of her instruction, only to be satisfied that she was doing much good, and that all who regard the future of the colored people in our country can select no better object for their charities than this school."

From Jasper Cope, of Philadelphia.

"I have been at the School for Colored Girls conducted under the management of Myrtilla Miner at Washington, D. C., and was much gratified with the degree and evidence of improvement in learning the scholars had arrived at ; and also pleased with the appearance of cleanliness in attire and the good order maintained throughout."

5th month, 1852.

From the Rev. Orville Dewey.

WASHINGTON, Jan. 27, 1853.

I entertain the most favorable opinion of Miss Miner's School for Colored Girls in this city, and of her ability, judgment and merit every way as a Teacher. I have visited her school several times and see it constantly improving. It is really an attractive spectacle—bright faces—an appearance of as much intelligence as I see in any other Schools—as quick and ready answers to questions—as much neatness, order and good behaviour. The School too is permanently established, and by no cause that I can foresee, is it likely to be disturbed or broken up.

There may be questions about the Slave System in America, but there can be no question about improving and elevating the free colored people by every wise means ; and I have no sympathy with him who can look upon Miss Miner's effort, I will not say with apathy, but without lively interest. ORVILLE DEWEY.

WASHINGTON, Dec. 23, 1853.

It gives me great pleasure to state that, from all that I have heard of the School of Miss Miner for Colored Children in this city, I am persuaded that she is accomplishing an excellent work in a quiet and unobjectionable manner, and that she deserves aid and sympathy in her effort to improve this much neglected portion of the population of our city. To this statement, my wife, who has visited the School and examined its pupils, desires to add her cordial and emphatic testimony.

C. M. BUTLER,
Rector of Trinity Church, Washington, D. C.

From Professor Horsford, of Cambridge University.

I was present at a morning exercise of Miss Miner's School for Colored Girls in Washington, during the winter of 1852-53.

The pupils present were of various ages from eight to sixteen years, and were plainly but neatly and comfortably clad. They consisted of mulattoes and quadroons for the most part, though some were obviously of pure African blood, and others could with difficulty be distinguished from whites.

The exercises were in spelling, reading, geography, penmanship, composition, analysis of authors, moral philosophy and translations from the French. The degree of attainment some had made, the manifest interest of all, and the prevailing healthful moral and religious tone were such, as to show that the School had been eminently successful. This is true, whether considered in view of its effects upon those who receive the instruction, or upon the families whose homes will be made happier, by the light that will accompany the knowledge thus imparted, or that circle of larger, if not indefinite extent, which will be blessed by the indirect influence of such an institution.

Few out of Washington can duly estimate the difficulties of organizing and sustaining there such a School. It requires on the part of its head, the rarest union of qualifications. There must be, beside varied accomplishments, the more important good sense, discretion, tact and energy, which wait upon all successful enterprises. In addition to these, Miss Miner has the deep religious faith, that united with other attributes, gives the fullest assurance, that while her life and health are continued, the school must prosper. I do not hesitate to add, that I have never attended a School exercise that interested me more deeply than that of Miss Miner's at Washington, nor can I escape the conviction that if the School can be maintained, its usefulness in the great cause of humanity will be more marked than if the pupils were white instead of colored.

Cambridge, Dec. 28, 1853. E. N. HORSFORD.

WASHINGTON, Jan. 7th, 1854.

It gives me high pleasure to express the satisfaction which I felt, in seeing the proofs of intelligence, good feeling and earnest desire to learn, manifested by Miss Miner's pupils at Washington ; and I congratulate her heartily on the growth and prosperity of her school.

The plan of establishing in the capital of the nation a Normal School for colored teachers, is admirable, alike for its originality and for its good sense and humanity. Here is the place to demonstrate by culture, their intellectual and moral power, and thus justify their aspirations for refinement and usefulness.

May the Teachers here instructed be powerful instruments in the peaceful solution of our great National Problem. With cordial respect and best wishes, W. H. CHANNING.

WASHINGTON, D. C., Jan. 7th, 1854.

I take pleasure in bearing testimony to the success of Miss Miner in her School of Colored Girls. I have twice visited the School ; and have been gratified with the proficiency of the pupils, not only in the elementary branches of education, but in the advanced studies. With some of the parents of these girls, (many of them enterprising and intelligent men,) I am intimately acquainted. Their honorable and Christian aspirations for the improvement of their daughters, and their deep interest in this School, are a sufficient guarantee of its character and worth. No highminded citizen of Washington I am assured can do otherwise than wish every possible success to this unobtrusive and philanthropic effort to in prove that portion of our population to whom we owe so large a debt.

I add also that Mrs. Sampson, who has likewise visited Miss Miner's School, has received the same favorable impression.

GEO. W. SAMPSON,
Pastor of the E. St. Baptist Church

PHILADELPHIA, 1mo. 23d, 1854.

In the winter of 1853, accompanied by a friend, I visited the School of Myrtilla Miner, under circumstances of peculiar interest.

Arriving about 10 A. M., we learned from a pupil at the door, that the teacher was absent on business of importance to the School.

We were not a little disappointed, supposing all recitations would await her coming. What was our surprise on entering, to find every pupil in her place, closely occupied with her studies. We seated ourselves by polite invitation — soon a class read—then one in Mental Arithmetic exercised itself, the more advanced pupils acting as monitors ; all was done without confusion. When the teacher entered she expressed no surprise but took up the business where she found it, and went on.

We learned subsequently, that this was no unusual thing. On one occasion, being obliged to leave for several days, she referred to the scholars the question, whether the house should be closed, or they continue their exercises without her—they chose the latter. On her return she found all doing well, not the least disorder having occurred.

A variety of testimony having been given respecting the intellectual attainments of the pupils, I deem it unnecessary to speak upon that topic ; but such instances as the above of self control, (that most difficult lesson to learn) suggest the previous history of the School, and afford an earnest of what may be expected in the future. MARGARET ROBINSON